PRAISE FOR CYNTHIA FREEMAN

"I have met and worked with a number of coaches over the years. Never have I encountered a more talented coach than Cynthia Freeman. Not only highly experienced, she is smart, insightful, and motivating. Cynthia's authenticity and professional competence are the result of her clear embodiment of the principles she coaches, enabling her to easily identify areas in which a client may be stuck and then quickly creating the strategies for breakthroughs."

—Carol Dawley

Managing Partner, JBD Capital

"I wanted to email you to say a huge "Thank you"! for all you did to make our nine days a truly rewarding, fun and inspiring experience. You were a great motivator and wonderful support—your wisdom, encouragement and caring really held our group together and the whole experience was better for your presence."

—Louise Hoskin

"I have been very impressed by Cynthia's ability to manage, organize, and create magic with a big group of people. Her leadership skills and experience pushed us to accomplish great things as a team as well as individually, while feeling very empowered to give the best of yourselves and be proud to get things done!"

—Francis Gendron

Founder of Solution ERA

"Cynthia is caring, empathetic, and has a high level of energy. She has the ability to motivate others and is an excellent leader. I would strongly recommend her to anyone interested in additional coaching and increasing their leadership skills."

—Bob McCabe

"Cynthia is a master motivator. Her unique blend of 'been there-done that' is an invaluable resource to anyone lucky enough to receive her guidance. Let her help you, because she can."

—Roger Love

World-Renown Celebrity Voice and Speaking Coach

www.RogerLove.com

"Getting coached by Cynthia Freeman has been like strapping on a jetpack, propelling my coaching business forward with huge momentum, in a way that would not have been possible by myself. The ride? Exciting, exhilarating and fun, and I knew at all times exactly how and where I would land! The power of Cynthia's wisdom, guidance and enthusiastic energy that she brings to each and every coaching session is one of the best experiences of my life! Thank you Cynthia."

—Sally Holden
Options for Life, Wagga Wagga, Australia

"Cynthia Freeman is one of those rare individuals who was 'coaching' before anyone coined the term. I've personally known Cynthia for well over a decade through our shared experiences in supporting Tony Robbins' live events. Cynthia has been a Sr. Trainer for Robbins Research International for 12 years. After moving to southern California and connecting at countless ICF events, we became close friends. While most of my 'Masters of Coaching' guests are more visibly known in the coaching community, I wanted Cynthia Freeman as a featured guest for numerous reasons.

"First, she is one of the most experienced coaches I know, touting over 17 years of experience working with people and companies in 51 different countries. Secondly, she is an MCC who has created TWO different coaching curriculums for business. She's also a rarity in earning her MCC without having graduated from an accredited coaching school (which is one of the most challenging ways to earn an MCC). She brings a unique perspective because of her longevity in the industry, and breadth of knowledge in working with individuals and organization on the topics of leadership, sales success, team building, teaching your children about money and more."

—Mary Allen

Author of *The Power of Inner Choice*

Professional Life & Business Coach

www.LifeCoachMary.com

"Cynthia Freeman has been coaching me since August 2014 and during that period, I have seen a dramatic improvement in my coaching skills. Most importantly, as a result my clients have managed to achieve their desired outcomes much faster. To this day, I am still in constant contact with Cynthia and my check points with her help me become the best coach I can be for my clients, employers, and community. Cynthia has encouraged and helped me on my journey to ICF accreditation. Her patience and direct approach in coaching me is the best tonic to get me moving! It doesn't matter that we are 15,000 km apart, she is always there to support my journey in becoming a coach."

—Kevin Kan

CEO, Break Out Consulting Asia

"I write and edit for a *lot* of very successful business people and thought leaders, and the tools and background I've gotten from working on Cynthia's book are *powerful*—I now use them every day. The Target Plan and the Five Star Formula, as well as a new understanding of where coaching fits and what it can do, have been a tremendous side-benefit of having the chance to work with Cynthia Freeman. And having the good luck to get to know her made it even better. I'll always be proud and grateful! Great book—read it, use it!"

—Rodney Miles

Editor-in-Chief, Rodney Miles Book Creation

www.RodneyMiles.com

"Having the opportunity to be coached by someone as knowledgeable as Cynthia Freeman has helped me to not only fine tune my skills as a coach but also improve my ability to approach clients and build a business. Cynthia's ability to really listen and analyze my coaching skills is fantastic. Cynthia delivers her advice and experience in a kind, loving and supportive way. Being a veteran in the coaching industry, what she has to share is invaluable. In the short time that I have been coached by Cynthia each session I grow and learn both professionally and personally. I would highly recommend anyone coaching to be coached by Cynthia as she is truly amazing."

—Vanessa Oldham
Personal Life Coach

THE POWER OF DONE

ALSO BY CYNTHIA FREEMAN

Money Does Grow on Trees

THE POWER OF DONE

Effective Strategies for Coaches,
Consultants, and C-Level Execs

CYNTHIA FREEMAN

For information about special discounts for bulk purchases
or author interviews, appearances, and speaking engagements
please contact:

www.CynthiaFreeman.com
Cynthia@CynthiaFreeman.com
P.O. Box 1001
Newport Beach, CA 92659
(424) 772-1776 Office Landline

First Edition

Written with the help of; cover and book design
by Rodney Miles: www.RodneyMiles.com
Edited by Dana Nichols: DanaNichols8@gmail.com
Personality Profile © Copyright 2001 Dynamic Life Design
18th Century Town Car (coach image)
http://www.georgianindex.net/horse_and_carriage/town-coach.gif

To my dad, Stanley Cramer,
who was tough while loving
and influenced so many lives.

And to my children
Brittany Renae and David Michael,
who lived through my trials and triumphs
and were my first "clients."

They made me the coach I am.

What lies behind us and what lies before us
are tiny matters compared to
what lies within us.
—OLIVER WENDELL HOLMES

To have an extraordinary quality of life

you need two skills:

the science of achievement

and the art of fulfillment.

—TONY ROBBINS

The Power of Done helps you do BOTH!

GET YOUR FREE BONUS!

In appreciation of your buying and reading this book, and as an encouragement of your success as a coach and in your life, please accept these free bonuses I have arranged for you.

Visit this page today!

http://www.cynthiafreeman.com/get-your-free-bonus/

Contents

ABOUT THIS BOOK

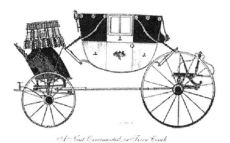

A Neat Constructed, or Town Coach

IN ADDITION TO BEING a resource for coaches, this book should prove very helpful for HR professionals and general managers who want to make something of their team and want help. Of course, however, this book should prove invaluable for those seeking to make coaching their avocation or vocation. It should put various systems you can use in different situations depending on what your clients are going through, that you can help them with.

ABOUT THE CARRIAGE

A Neat Ornamented, or Town Coach

ORIGINALLY WE HAD A cover design that included a large check mark, and we liked it for some time. But after some thought, we removed it, and it was a blessing in actuality. It took writing the whole book to crystallize this— the carriage *and coaching* is about *moving forward*, not "checking off boxes," as they say.

It's something I've learned in my life and in my career. It's more than ticking a box—the *power of done* is the power of moving your life forward.

3

GET YOUR FREE BONUS!

In appreciation of your buying and reading this book, and as an encouragement of your success as a coach and in your life, please accept these free bonuses I have arranged for you. Visit this page today!

http://www.cynthiafreeman.com/get-your-free-bonus/

PART 1: THIS IS COACHING

COACH DEFINED

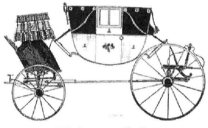

A Neat Ornamented, x Town Coach

coach[1]

/kōCH/

noun

noun: **coach**; plural noun: **coaches**

1. a horse-drawn carriage, especially a closed one.

2. a railroad car.

- NORTH AMERICAN

economy class seating in an aircraft or train.

noun: **coach class**

3. a bus, especially one that is comfortably equipped and used for longer journeys.

verb

verb: **coach**; 3rd person present: **coaches**; past tense: **coached**; past participle: **coached**; gerund or present participle: **coaching**

1. travel by coach.

adverb

- NORTH AMERICAN

adverb: **coach**

1. in economy class accommodations in an aircraft or train.

Origin

mid 16th century (sense 1 of the noun): from French *coche*, from Hungarian *kocsi* *(szekér)* '(wagon) from Kocs,' a town in Hungary.

coach²

kōCH/

noun

noun: **coach**; plural noun: **coaches**

1. an athletic instructor or trainer.

- a tutor who gives private or specialized teaching.

verb

verb: **coach**; 3rd person present: **coaches**; past tense: **coached**; past participle: **coached**; gerund or present participle: **coaching**

1. train or instruct (a team or player).
   - give (someone) extra or private teaching.
   - teach (a subject or sport) as a coach.
   - prompt or urge (someone) with instructions.

Origin

early 18th century (as a verb): figuratively from coach¹.

WHY COACHING?

A Neat Ornamented, or Town Coach

I WAS IN THIS PROFESSION before it had a name, before it was called "coaching." I believe in this as a career. I see coaching as a real force that can make a change for people in whatever they are doing. But I didn't start out to be a coach.

Born and bred in southern California, I grew up in La Habra, which is the home of the Hass avocado (where Rudolph Hass planted the Hass Avocado Mother Tree in the 1920s, the Hass avocado becoming one of the most popular in the world). It's the one everyone loves the most. It's not the best looking—it's kind of dark and nubby—but it's got the meatiest flesh inside. Very famous.

I'm the granddaughter of ranchers who grew the region's original lemon, orange, and avocado groves. The ranches are not there anymore—in fact, the last ranches fell in the early 2000s—and have been replaced by homes. Fallbrook, California is now the "Avocado Capital" of the world, along with certain regions of Mexico.

BROKEN CLIPBOARDS

And I probably became a coach, ultimately, because my dad was a football coach, eventually the head football coach for Mt. San Antonio College in Walnut, Calif. Now, as a football coach, Dad modeled how to influence, inspire, train, and discipline on the football field, and I use these tactics today in another realm. I really became "my father's daughter" and I do think there is a lot of influence from Dad having been a coach. In fact, that is why I started calling what I do "coaching": because I realized that I was doing what Dad did with his players.

Before his coaching days, Dad had been a football player for the University of Southern California. He actually played in a Rose Bowl with them and he was actually drafted into the

NFL but he didn't go. My mother was not about to move to Green Bay! Mom and Dad were died-in-the-wool southern Californians, with all their family and friends here. They were not moving to ice and snow. Mom had lived through the war and gotten my dad back, and we were certainly not going to Wisconsin. In looking back, it all happened the way it was supposed to happen.

In one of my favorite childhood pictures, my sister and Dad sit with a wood board that he used for coaching. It had a football field painted on it with players made out of the tops of clothes hangers. He would move the players around and figure out all these plays. It was so cute. We would watch him move them around to go through the motions in three dimensions. Now, this was in the sixties! You had to do it all on a chalkboard normally, but here he could figure out these plays and translate it all into plays he could call with his guys, like a big chessboard. It made it way more real than X's and O's and lines. You can *demonstrate* that way. No idea when he came up with that, but I was probably in kindergarten when he had that thing.

I will never forget that Dad was an assistant coach when I was five years old, the same year I had the wonderful experience of breaking my arm on a New Year's Day. No matter the reason, it's not a good thing to take your football coach dad away from the televised football games on New

Year's Day and have to go to the hospital. I don't think I ever lived that down.

In fact when I had my cast off my arm I would have to go to the whirlpool at the gym with the football players. At home I had two little sisters and these guys were like my big brothers. There I'd be, this little squirt dangling her atrophied arm among big football players nursing sore knees.

The football players would come to the house, eat with us, throw me in the air—they were my big brothers. My mom would drive us to practices and we would watch them drill over and over. Dad had his whistle around his neck and he had his stopwatch, which I still have today. He had his clipboard, with the plays, I guess, and we would watch them practice. I can remember as the guys were running back and forth, doing sprints and so on, that we would want to be as good as these guys, my sisters and I. We were Coach's daughters, right? We would run and run, and watch them practice over and over.

Every Saturday night we were at the games. Not just the home games, either. We went to every single game. Honestly, I remember watching Dad on the sidelines. I remember when he was excited, how he would really encourage these guys and cheer them on, how he'd give them pats on the back and the high-fives, and the hugs. I also remember him getting upset.

And here's what's really interesting. He would never get upset at the players. He would get upset with himself. You could tell what kind of a night it had been if the clipboard came home in one piece or if it was broken. Seriously. Dad could access his frustration very easily, hence the broken clipboard. If one of his players did something very stupid that clipboard got trashed. Sometimes he broke the clipboard on the field, and sometimes he broke it in the locker room. The point is that he never took it out on any one kid. He released his frustration, and then got back to the plan.

"Okay guys. Now we have to get back to what we're going to do," he'd say.

I think as a coach myself, I get upset with *me*, not at my clients if they are not getting results. I have a couple clients right now, in fact, who are in real estate and I get upset if they're not getting the results I think they ought to be getting because they're putting in the time and they're doing the part they're supposed to be doing. I rack my brain and ask myself questions such as, "What else could I help them with? What else could I give them insight on? What else can I add?"

What I remember most about my dad is the influence he had on individual guys' lives, particularly those who had terrible family lives and literally weren't fed at home. Dad would invite them into our home for meals and study time. Even though we lived on one coach's salary, we were ranchers so we always had food. These huge guys had all this talent and no wherewithal, no encouragement at home, and no food. They needed to eat, and they needed somebody to tell them they were talented and could do anything and achieve their goals. They needed someplace to get away from the craziness so they could study. And I remember sitting around the table studying with them. These guys, one by one, they became like my brothers. Sometimes they were there in twos and threes, sometimes just one.

It started with one young man in particular, his name was Ray Aderman, and he was an all-American football player. He went on to a full scholarship at college, based on Dad's encouragement, my dad's coaching of him, and Dad getting him out of the slums. He became like a big brother or uncle in my own life.

And Dad kept in touch with all of these guys. Some of them went on to coach at major universities. I remember Bob Stillwell went on to coach at Ohio University—I could go on and on. These guys who Dad really took in and put under his wing to give them a better opportunity at life, they went on to not only graduate from a four-year school, but to have successful careers and none of them, none of them, ever got into trouble. They all led stellar lives.

Encouraging his players and living by example -- going to work and working diligently -- is what it took to succeed.

But I don't want to say working "hard"—Dad did work hard, don't get me wrong, and I was raised on that strong work ethic—but he showed these guys more: he'd take them camping, take them to church, and show them little pieces of life. He showed them how to be men. Yes, he coached them in football but he coached them to be *outstanding citizens*. I know how they were being raised and I know the families and neighborhoods they came out of, and they all would have otherwise gotten into trouble, every one of them. We had every size, shape, color, creed, and everything, and they were awesome, and I love that about my parents, they taught us "We are people, all of us, all the same." It was about *character*. Dad was an example for them and he helped them. He had a strong belief that his guys should get punished not for bad plays, but for demonstrating bad character. The truth is, as a collegiate coach, that is what you should be teaching the kids.

Today I love college football. I am so excited when college football starts, but the NFL today breaks my heart. I don't mind it being a business, but I mind it *just* being a business. It affects our culture as a whole when the presence of good character is weak or missing.

Dad went on years later to become the Dean of Counseling and Guidance at the college. And when he passed in 2012, there must have been over a thousand people at the funeral. I swear—half of them were his former players. They testified to how he changed their lives, how he influenced them and the choices they made, how he influenced the careers they'd gone into, and who they became as men and fathers. Pretty amazing. It was a real testimony to a successful coach. Whether you are a life coach, a business coach, or a personal coach, to hear someone say, "You have influenced who I have become as a father and a businessman," is the ultimate reward.

It was pretty remarkable for me, to see that testimony there, and what a turnout! We were stunned. My only regret is it wasn't recorded. I wish so much we had recorded all those testimonies, just one after the other. These big former football players, now grandfathers themselves, had grown to become incredible, successful men. It was amazing. Dad played a profound role in that.

A SURVIVOR AND A FIGHTER

One more thing about Dad: my mother sort of knew this but we were never allowed to know about his experience in World War II, from which he came back victimized to a terrible degree. He had been a sergeant of an entire unit of machine gun soldiers. He actually told my son this story, and my son was so affected by it he only shared the framework and not the greater detail. The story is as follows: Dad was to the rear of Patton in a campaign in the European theater. Patton was known for bloody battles, too. Being in the rear of Patton was gruesome, it was brutal. And not every battle went well. The reason we won is Patton took risks. With great risks there is opportunity for great rewards, but with great risk there can be great loss. My dad's detail at one point in Germany lost every man in his unit except him. Somehow, miraculously, he came back. And that's what enables me to do what I do. I don't take that lightly. This was shared at my dad's funeral. His fight for survival enabled him to touch each of his players by taking them under his wing, caring for them and helping them becoming contributing citizens; and it allowed me to live and thrive during a golden age in the United States. I was raised in a great upper-middle-class setting, achieved a university education, and have had the opportunity to influence lives the way I do today.

If that story had gone differently and he had not become the man he had become... The truth is he became a survivor and a fighter, and a real strong, hard worker out of that horrible atrocity, and I got to model that. Many people have seen some of the crummy things I have gone through in my own life—and believe me, there have been bad times, a few years in particular that were a very icky season—and my friends have said to me, "Cynthia, you're a survivor." And I know where I get it. One hundred percent.

MOVEMENT THERAPY

My university studies were in movement therapy and dance (bachelor's degree), and I have a masters degree in what we would today call movement psychology. Interestingly, these studies have really influenced my coaching, because motion creates emotion.

Out of college I entered the medical field and I realized, as doctors and I were treating patients, that not only was a lot of transference influencing doctors, but that we could not change the past for our patients. And with what we were doing we could not really influence the future, either. To influence the future, you would have to change what you were and what you valued, change your identity and all of that to actually move you forward. So I got out of that field, and got into real estate to make a living.

200 HOUSES

I ran a very successful real estate business beginning in 1979. I certainly did everything poorly, initially, but by reading and getting training, I got very good at what I did, selling 10 to 15 houses per year. But by getting on purpose and getting some training, through study and deciding to run things as a business as opposed to a hobby, I became very successful. And after initially selling around 10 houses each year, with these changes I went on to selling 51 deals the very next year, 90-something the year after that, and something over 200 the year after that.

It involved having a staff and assistants, and running a system-based operation. My marketing was very cutting edge. And that's what really helped me accomplish what I did with my business. It helped me also get noticed and start having others come to me to learn what it was I was doing.

I was a single mom with two little kids. For twelve years I had been by myself, since they were ages one and three, and believe me, I started to starve initially and had to figure out how to do this. So in the meantime people were calling me from all over the place to pick my brain. It caused me to figure out what my recipe was and I helped those people replicate what I was doing.

Here's the story of how my career in coaching came out of my learning curve in real estate:

YOUR SECOND HALF

I figured out strategies. I created a plan and followed the plan and got it done. I changed my focus and my self-talk and shifted my identity to get things done and make that happen.

And in real estate I went from being a salesperson to a professional real estate guru because of strategies, a plan, and following a plan. What this represents is my Target Plan and my Five Star Formula. When you use those two strategies, things get DONE! The essence, and what was replicatable was I changed my strategies, then my focus then my identity and things got done. Others I knew in real estate *knew* real estate, but they didn't know this, about this process. I therefore don't call myself a "coach," I call myself a professional life strategist.

So many people go into careers just the way I went into real estate, because others tell you that you'd be good at something, that it's actually one of the reasons I became a coach. Eventually I went from exclusively being a real estate agent to being a real estate agent as well as the regional trainer, which was my natural bent. A revelatory moment came when I was in a class training new people and asking them how they came to be in real estate. As they answered, I realized I had really not asked myself that question. One girl explained she had read a book called *What Color is Your Parachute?* which was so new at the time that I had not yet heard of it. She said to me, "It asked me this whole list of questions and by the end it was obvious to me I should be a real estate agent!"

It caused me to get the book. All it took was my reading and asking myself internally, without even writing anything down, the first five questions. They dealt with things like, "Why are you in this business?" and "How did you happen to choose this?" and all about your past careers. In my head I realized I had gotten into real estate to support myself. I didn't know what else to do at the time. In fact everyone else—my mother, my boyfriend, my best friend—all said, "You would be so great in real estate! You should go into it!" And I realized I went into real estate simply based on the opinions from all of these people, because I respected them and their views.

But none of the reasons were *my* reasons. None of it had to do with what I liked, what I myself chose, what I wanted. None of it had anything to do with *me*.

"Oh my gosh," I said, "Here I am in a field to make everybody else happy." And real estate had become so litigious at that time and place, that everyone was out to sue you, and the more successful you were, the more they wanted your wealth and felt you didn't deserve it. I can remember to this day the clients' names and addresses associated with two particular deals that slaughtered me emotionally. I was done. I made a decision. I was not going to sell myself short to make a dollar—ever. I decided I had to do something for myself, for *my* reasons.

And that's tough! I was 40 years old when I got into the business of coaching. That's generally not the time one is recommended to change careers! But here's the truth: statistically, it is, in fact, the best time, because once you've had some life experience, that experience is terribly valuable. If you get on purpose and you focus—and I know because I've lived it and I've helped others live it too—your second half can be *way* better than your first half. Absolutely.

I have to say that if could I do it all over, if I had the coaching skills then that I have now, I would have done it with a better plan and strategy. But I will say that I've made six figures in two careers at this point, and as a single female that's not just pretty good, it's pretty rare.

Having raised two kids and having put work first most of the time (in my defense, I became quite adept at "balance"), there's a lot I would do differently today. And I think my daughter can see that I really am taking time off and maneuvering things around these days. It's not that I'm quitting coaching, but I have to say that I am choosing to be a grandmother who is really all-in. I'm doing stuff that neither my mother nor my mother-in-law did for me—only because in some way I'm going to make up for what I didn't do for my kids. And you know what? I think that's okay. You get a second chance in your personal life as well to make a different choice.

WOMEN

As a woman, I will say that conditions for us in this country have gotten 100% better and are getting better every day. Opportunities continue opening up. In fact I have a client whose business focuses on bridging the gender gap in pay. It's a very current topic internationally, and she's not alone in what she's doing. There are now international forums about that.

Look at some of the huge tech companies: who's in charge or has been recently of Google? eBay? Hewlett Packard? These seats are now occupied or have been occupied by women who are all in their fifties. I'm a fan, in fact, of Carly Fiorina. Her 2016 presidential run was inspiring for what it brought to the conversation. Just to hear her speak about what she believes should happen to improve things is inspiring.

But these women who are running things, who are influencing things, please note that they are all doing this in their second halves of their lives. They are not twenty-somethings who are running around doing all of this. It proves to me that, gosh, you can start again! I'm encouraging my daughter right now, who just had my first grandbaby, who looks like he'll be a linebacker one day, by the way, and she looks to me like she's realizing, "Wow, this is my life!" What I tell her is this is a *piece* of her life.

My mother comes into the picture as another good example. She raised us kids until my youngest sister was in high school. My mother then went back to get her master's degree. It led her to *starting* the Oral History Department at a university. It's one of the premier oral history programs in the world. She's written a first book and working on another. She became the executive vice president of a huge marketing chain. She's a judge for the Pillsbury bake-off and in charge of their consumer affairs for the U.S. And she didn't start any of that until she was in her forties. She had an entire life before her second half. And I'm doing the same, to be honest.

THE DAWN OF COACHING

You can give people systems but that won't make them successful. In fact you can teach somebody how to run a business and have systems in place and so on but that's not what makes them successful. I had really learned how to manage my state, how to shift my identity, how to manage my resources, and how to juggle everything when I was selling real estate. I don't actually believe that perfect balance is possible but I do believe you can learn how to run things so you don't also run yourself into the ground, and how to own a business and not be owned by one. And that's how I started helping people. They were then able to be more successful by implementing my ideas.

"Coaching" as it is today was a fascinating thing to watch organically evolve. We called it other things before we called it coaching, and it seemed that it came to be called "coaching" just out of the blue at one point. Back then, on the road with Tony Robbins, we didn't have anything called coaching but we had what we called a "strategy session" that upsold people into an entire package of Tony Robbins services. We were, in fact, actually coaching people— coaching them in some particular aspect or the broad scope of their lives.

Tony didn't call himself a "coach" even though he and I had been coaching, really, since 1991. We called it "business consulting" or an even bigger term, "business planning." I called myself a business consultant initially in 1991. But by the end of the 1990s Tony realized that what we were doing—as opposed to being a motivational speaker as Tony described himself—was being *peak performance coaches*. And from that point on, Tony for years and years corrected people again and again, that he was not a "motivational speaker," that he was in fact a coach. When coaching really caught on in the late 1990s, Tony decided to create an arm of his company in which he trained coaches—I was one of them.

At my second Tony Robbins seminar over in Hawaii in 1995, there were people there calling themselves coaches. People would tell me they had just joined the International Coaches Federation, for example. Thomas Leonard, Sandy Vilas, Cheryl Richardson, and other people who were all forerunners in the field, were kind of running things. My view was "Who put them in charge? We're all coaching here, and why do we need to go to them to be certified?" I was shortsighted, though, and two years later joined the ICF.

The American Medical Association, for example, started the same way. There were these wagons with elixirs running wild around the country and they realized back then, "Hey, we need standards and a code of conduct, and to instill ethics." Well, I wanted the same thing for this career path I had taken a shift into.

As a Coach

By 1995 I was full-time as a coach and by 1997 I was certified and have been a certified master coach with the ICF for all these years. It's not the only organization, nor a perfect one, but it is international. What's great is there is now a set of standards agreed to around the world and it is beneficial to everyone to have some semblance of standards and ethics.

As I got into coaching I realized everything I learned in college courses on movement therapy (I still have all the books!) was of use. All of the coaching seminar leaders I encountered—whether it was Harvey Mackay, Tom Hopkins, Tony Robbins, or one of my all time favorites, Zig Ziglar— seemed to reference the books I'd read in college! Zig Ziglar, by the way, was the first motivational speaker I saw speak live to an audience. Truly, at the root of who he is, Zig Ziglar was an awesome coach, as I reflect back and look at what he taught. But it was so funny to circle back around to my entire education and realize, "Okay, I can use all of that now!" Nothing from real estate was wasted, either. In fact, all the years I did it poorly and then did it well and then did it outstanding, all of that knowledge was now getting used. I use all of those pieces in my coaching even now, every day.

I had a BA and an MA from a major university, and I had some business acumen, having seen what worked and what didn't work as a real estate agent, even though it wasn't what I studied in college. All these experiences led to my current business, Dynamic Life, which is very much about the second half of life, as its being a whole new opportunity, just as Dad would have coached his young men. I now help people do what they want to do and become what they want to become, and I do it as a coach.

COACHING TODAY

A Neat Ornamented, or Town Coach

THE USE OF THE word "coach" (not capitalized) along the upper line in the graph that follows on page 24 and "Coach" (capitalized) in the lower line of the graph as found in scanned books according to Google, are on the rise, and more so as a capitalized term (source: Google Books Ngram Viewer).

EXPLODING GROWTH

Coaching in one form or another, according to the preceding graph, is ostensibly on the rise. It could mean both life and athletic coaches are growing in significance in modern society, and even so, this might suggest we are becoming generally more aware of what role coaching can play in our own lives and careers. It's a good thing.

According to surveys, coaching in large corporate environments is on a very quick increase, with a majority of all companies surveyed both believing it is a key component of development and actually using it, along with using some form of team building.[1]

In 2007 there were an estimated 40,000 life and business coaches in the United States, and it was a $2.4 billion-dollar industry, growing at a pace of 18% each year.[2] Indeed, a career as a professional coach has become more needed, wanted, and highly regarded, and the number of those calling themselves professional coaches has been on a significant rise over the last 15 years.[3]

---

[1] http://en.wikipedia.org/wiki/Coaching
[2] "Statistics". Business coaching. 29 October 2009. Retrieved 28 March 2012.
[3] "Coach Career Survey". SolutionBox. 2007.

The following chart shows use of the terms "coach" and "Coach" on upward trends since the 1980s.

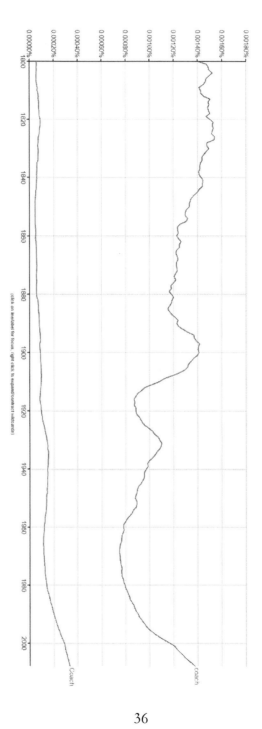

This is, for many, in large part thanks to Thomas J. Leonard. Author of seven books on the subject, Thomas J. Leonard played a significant role in the development of personal coaching and founded both Coach University in 1992 and the International Coach Federation in 1994, as well as other important organizations. He passed away in 2003.[4]

BUT WHAT IS IT?

But what is it? What exactly is coaching? One definition is, "a training or development process via which an individual is supported while achieving a specific personal or professional competence result or goal."[5] Intuitive, and applicable of course to all sorts of areas, relationships, your career, sports, or actually anything that involves accomplishment. There are people who can help you get there. The next assumption might be that there are various techniques of coaching, and there indeed are, some better than others. The relationship can be formal or casual, of course, but "coaching," according to the above definition which is broadly accepted, denotes and includes the specific achievement of some result or competence. Compare this to "mentoring," which implies more general development by following the examples and

---

[4] http://www.coachville.com/tl/thomasleonard/bio.html
[5] http://en.wikipedia.org/wiki/Coaching

guidance of someone presumably more experienced and expert in the desired area(s) of accomplishment.

And specifically, regardless of the method employed, coaching seeks to achieve new ways of thinking by the recipient as well as establishing new behaviors, all of which should lead to personal growth and/or professional advancement, and in the case of an athletic coach, an actual physical skill.

I have always found the derivations of words, etymology, to be very revealing, and that of the term for my own profession is no exception. The word "coach" derives from the Hungarian word *kocsi*, which is a carriage, named after the village in which it was first made. And this is so incredibly applicable to what we do as coaches, we carry something from one place to another. A coach believes in someone before they ever believe in themselves. I know what a client can do, I know what they can make happen, before they ever believe in themselves.

"Coach" was used around 1830 as a term for instruction or training at Oxford as slang for a tutor who "carries" a student through an exam. This actually predates the first known use in 1861 of the term as applied to athletics. In all cases, the concept is of bringing someone from a place or position to another place or position they desire to be.

Managing is making sure people do what they know how to do. Training is teaching people to do what they don't know how to do. Mentoring is showing people how the people who are really good at doing something do it. Counseling is helping people come to terms with issues they are facing. Coaching is none of these – it is helping to identify the skills and capabilities that are within the person, and enabling them to use them to the best of their ability.

Professional coaching uses a range of communication skills (such as targeted restatements, listening, questioning, clarifying etc.) to help clients shift their perspectives and thereby discover different solutions to achieve their goals.[6]

Personal and professional coaching is then, kind of three feet behind everything else, as sort of a modern "profession of professions" as it applies to and assists practically all human endeavors.

HISTORY

While the concept and practice of coaching in various forms has been used throughout history and we can trace its more recent appearance in the 1800s in various forms, it seems to

---

[6] Cox, E (2013), *Coaching Understood*, London: Sage.

appear in more organized and popular forms in the early 1970s Human Potential Movement and numerous self-help groups and studies at the time. One of these groups, who was focused on EST training, was founded by Werner Erhard, who led his group throughout the 1970s and 1980s and is often credited with being one of the first people to use the term "coaching" in relation to personal development.7 Timothy Galloway is credited as being a pioneer in first using formal coaching as a comprehensive approach to sports and team development, versus it being more simply a transference of skills from one expert to a protégé.

Coaching really seemed to get codified and gain recognition as an independent practice in the mid-1990s with the popping up of professional organizations, including:

- Association for Coaching
- The International Coach Federation
- European Coaching and Mentoring Council

As I mentioned in the previous chapter, such organizations compile and introduce standards followed by

---

[7] Morgan, Spencer (27 January 2012), "Should a Life Coach Have a Life First", *The New York Times.*

40

members and help elevate practices to the level of professionalism and high ethics.

Today coaching is divided into various arenas including:

- Life coaching
- Executive coaching
- Wealth coaching
- Emotional intelligence coaching
- and others

TYPES AND STYLES

Socrates might approve of modern coaching, as a popular form of coaching involves the asking of questions and then providing opportunities for the recipient or "coachee" to come to his or her own conclusions. The advantage can be that when one arrives at such conclusions oneself, they include that person's specific life experience, culture, values and views.

LIFE COACHING

To help people identify and achieve their personal goals a life coach may employ intelligence and techniques from the fields of sociology, neuroscience, career counseling, psychology and other fields. They may further specialize in particular facets of personal life and use techniques that include hypnosis Neuro Linguistic Programming, affirmations, marketing and dream analysis, while not necessarily being a therapist, athletic trainer, business consultant, or health care professional per se. For example, *ADHD coaching* is a highly specialized form of life coaching. In practice, life coaches should practice clarity in disseminating what it is they do and don't do for clients, so there will be no confusion or construing what one does as some other licensed profession.

BUSINESS COACHING

Business coaching and its subsidiaries, leadership, executive, and corporate coaching, is part personal coaching and part human resource development. It generally includes support, feedback, and advice to both individuals and groups to improve efficiency and effectiveness at work.

Business coaching professionals can become members of and receive training from various professional associations and organizations:

- Professional Business Coach Alliance
- International Coach Federation

- International Coaching Council
- Worldwide Association of Business Coaches

And there's no one single, agreed-upon best method for business coaches, or as some call themselves, business consultants. Methods can vary widely and there is no requisite licensing for business coaches or consultants. Business coaching is one of the fastest growing professions in the world today.

OTHER COACHING TYPES

For every kind of need, there this a coach in today's world. Executives, those seeking career guidance, expatriates and global executives, those going through a divorce, those seeking help with their finances, athletes, those dealing with being a victim or in a conflict of some kind, and even students seeking help accomplishing more with homework, all have niche coaches and professionals available to them today.

Surely, there is a rewarding niche for *you as a coach* and those you help. I can tell you, the rewards of being a part of another's hard-won accomplishment can seem as great as having done it yourself.

GET YOUR FREE BONUS!

In appreciation of your buying and reading this book, and as an encouragement of your success as a coach and in your life, please accept these free bonuses I have arranged for you. Visit this page today!

http://www.cynthiafreeman.com/get-your-free-bonus/

PART 2: "CREATE IT," THE SEVEN KEYS OF COACHING

OVERVIEW: SEVEN KEYS

A Neat Ornamented, or Town Coach

IN THE 1970S, WITH A MASTERS DEGREE in movement therapy, I went to work as an adjunct therapist. I had done an internship and gotten the job. Coaching, per se, did not even exist at the time. I worked in a psychiatric facility and learned very quickly in charting patients that therapy definitely has a place—I really do believe in therapy—but it was only half the picture.

COACHING VERSUS THERAPY

I kept working with these patients who I felt were really more like clients, who should be considered more as clients whom you give tools and help, and get them to go out there and tackle the world. I have to add here that I believe we have developed a very soft culture of people who don't have emotional muscle, and I can give you lots of examples of this. Now, I don't believe that therapy causes that by any means but here's how I see therapy's place: I refer people out to a therapist if I believe they need to work on stuff that is in the rear view mirror.

When working with patients, I had this innate feeling that they could do a little therapy and get some tools and skills out of it that would prepare them for the next step. I think a great approach would be a therapist working with someone and then handing them off to a coach to help them then go out and tackle their *future*. And I don't see therapists helping people move into the future. I see them, really, trying to change the past. I've always known deep down that the past is not something you can change. To quote Tony Robbins, "The past doesn't equal the future." And if you think about it, that is so true. The past is the past. It is what it is and it may be ugly and awful and terrible, but it doesn't have to be what is true for tomorrow. In fact, you can get skills, tools and strategies to move into your future without dragging the past, strapped like a ball and chain to your ankle, along with you. This is what I believe coaches do -- they help people leave that behind and move ahead.

I do know that it takes some real work to do that, and coaching can absolutely do that. I realize there are therapists who want to help people *come to grips with the past so they can move forward.* So there is a place for therapy, where you go very deep, where you understand what happened, where you go into coping with trauma, tragedy or grief—and then there is a place for coaching.

Coaching gives and equips you with things to work on and move forward. It is very forward-facing. When I listen to other coaches coaching, I am very quick to point out when they are going into therapy by looking backwards. When they start analyzing and going through the past, I believe they are treading in therapeutic waters. And other than for a client to figure out why something happened, what was going on and what all that means, it doesn't have to have anything to do with the future. It's important to realize there is a real difference. Coaches can sometimes open up a can of worms if you've gone into therapeutic land and you're not equipped for that, and you really need to stay out of there. So I want to be very clear in saying I am not helping people to learn how to do therapy—that is not the skill set I am talking about here. We want to be cautious that if you're a coach, you are not doing therapy. That's very important. Let's also be clear that there's a liability in doing that.

THE SEVEN KEYS

Okay, so we now know we are not performing therapy, we are coaching and looking ahead. I have a system of ideas, of principles you should have as a coach. I believe there are *Seven Keys* to coaching. There are lots of places to go and get education for coaching. There are schools of coaching and they all have their own bent or platform and this book and my approach also have their own strategy of coaching. There are lots of really good ones, and I think it's important to realize that if you want the online kind of training there are things like CoachU, for example. There are others but CoachU was the first and is kind of the grandfather of coach training online. It started in the mid-1990s. There is also a very big proponent of proactive coaching, and that is CTI, Coaches Training Institute. And there are many more, but these, as good examples, each have a different frame of thought about how to go about coaching. There are lots of educational systems for coaching, and this Seven Keys approach of mine, is one.

There are also organizations you can belong to and you can be certified by. At this moment, at this book's publishing it is not a requirement by law that you be certified. I personally am. I went with what I call the grandfather of organizations, which is the International Coach Federation (ICF). I am also a board certified coach, known as a BCC. There are several organizations you can belong to as a coach and be certified which adds to your credibility. The most important part of belonging to an organization for coaches for clients looking for a coach is that it declares a member coach has to abide by a code of ethics and morals. They have had to pass exams that speak to that, in fact. You know that these associations are focused on core competencies for coaching so there are some established standards. This is all a piece of what coaching is today.

EXPLORE AND EXAMINE

What I believe to be the Seven Keys to coaching fall into two phases. Phase One is exploring and examining. Phase Two is the step-by-step implementation. In Phase One, you are in a discovery process, learning about the client. Meanwhile the client is going through some self discovery, answering some powerful questions about what they really want, getting some clarity around that and developing the best strategies for them. At first, though, they have to understand who they are and what they believe. What do they value and how do they operate? And what's their modus operandi? What a coach is understanding in this exploring and examining section is who this client is and what they want to do.

The Seven Keys are made easy-to-remember by my acronym CREATE IT:

CREATE IT

1. **C**reate

   Relationship

2. **E**xplore

3. **A**ssess

4. **T**ransform

5. **E**xecute

6. **I**ntegrate & Celebrate

7. **T**ake Next Steps

Once you've got that understanding you will go through what I call *CREATE IT,* which is an acronym. In this second phase of process you're going to rewire and reset everything so it's going to operate the way you want it to operate. What we discover in the examination and exploration phase is, "Oh my gosh—I've got conflicting values," or "I've got conflicting beliefs. I'm trying to talk out of both sides of my mouth and trying to operate that way, I'm trying to go north and south at the same time."

It's interesting. We aren't born with an identity. We aren't born with beliefs, so it's important to explore, examine and discover what you do have there because that's your code of conduct. That's how you operate. It's based on those premises. And here's the discovery in coaching: You're not born with that. You actually, in fact develop it along the way. This includes the identity you hold. In other words, this actually includes who you say you are. Of course most people never stop and answer the question, "Who am I?" They're just operating from, "I'm this, I'm this, I'm not that. I'm good at throwing a ball, I'm horrible at throwing a ball, I'm great at math, I suck at math. I'm awesome at numbers, I can't deal with numbers. I'm great at finding my way through navigation, I couldn't find my way out of a paper bag."

Anytime you're saying "I am" or I am not" you're making a statement about your identity. Here's what people never stop and look at: You weren't born with that. Somehow, I would say one of the most revealing moments in my life was around 1993 when someone posed this in a seminar and I stood there and I realized something big. When I asked myself the questions, "Why do I believe that? Where did I get that?" I realized my own ideas of myself had come from all the people I respected: my parents, my grandparents, my best friends, my teachers, and so on. They were all well-meaning, but I had adopted *their* ideas of me. Why, for example, was I a real estate agent? Well because all these people who I counted on said I'd be really good at it.

So we formulate this identity and nobody ever stops and thinks, "Well, is that who you want to be? Is *that* person going to help you become and accomplish or achieve what you want to achieve? And the truth is, the answer might be yes and the answer might be no. But again, the great news is this:

You can create your own beliefs, values, and identity to be what serves you and are necessary to accomplish your goals.

You can create them. Look, you created it at one time! You created who you are *today* so you can actually create this again, and that is part of what coaching can help with. So we're going to rewire and reset so that they are who they want to be and they've got a system in place internally that is going to take them to the destination they want. Because really what we want to do is rewire and reset their operating system to get them the results they want in a way that they feel fulfilled and rewarded.

These, then, are the Seven Keys to coaching, and we'll expand on each of these in their own chapter. For starters, here's an overview of the Seven Keys. And it's easy to remember them with the acronym I have created: CREATE IT.

1. CREATE RELATIONSHIP

Create a Relationship. It's all about developing a rapport with your client. It means you develop a safe space to be real and open with them, really crack the code of who they've been, who they need to be, and what system they need to operate from in order to get the results they want to get in their life. Creating a relationship is really that foundation. It's the real fundamental laying of groundwork to then be able to partner, to work together, coach and client, to get to where you want to go.

2. EXPLORE

The second piece is the *explore* piece. What's important in this exploring is looking at all the aspects of who this person is, how they've been wired, how they've been operating, and how they've been trying, up until now, to get where they wanted to go.

3. ASSESS

Now we've got all these great assessments, so the next piece is assess. You're going to look at your client's strengths and limitations and have them ask, "Okay, have I been playing to my strengths too much? Are these limitations something I can mitigate?" You're going to assess all of these things. There are so many awesome tools out there for assessing. This is not the end-all, be-all of your practice, but this part of coaching is very valuable. You can look at levels of stress, how your client meets goals and so on.

I love Gary Chapman's book series, *Love Languages*—that is to say how you give and how you receive. When you're interacting with other people and we're in relationships in our lives, it's important to understand that the universe doesn't revolve around our particular style, so it's good to assess what works for us and to then be aware of what might work best for others. So assessing is very important.

4. TRANSFORM

Once you've assessed, obviously you're going to make a few tweaks. You're going to begin a *transformation*. You're going to decide what is going to change. You're going to decide how to make that change stick and stay so that your client can operate from a new frame, if that is what's going to serve them. That next step, then is to transform.

5. EXECUTE

Then you're going into *execution*. And with execution you've got a couple of different things, whether it's an emotional piece you need to transform, or how to actually achieve things in life, how to get to destinations in life, or how to accomplish the goals your client has set.

For this I've got systems that enable people to operate. One is the Five Star Formula and the other is the Target Plan, and we'll cover them both in this text. You want to help them have a system to execute in an effective and efficient fashion so they get what they really want instead of getting whatever is left over or whatever comes their way. You don't want an attitude of "whatever happens, happens," or "que sera sera," (whatever will be, will be). With what you're providing, people are going to have an ability to execute and in execution they're going to achieve what they want. And it's going to be *by design*.

6. INTEGRATE AND CELEBRATE

The sixth key is to integrate and celebrate. Without integration, it's all just a great idea, it's just something to look at and it sounds nice or it looks nice, but it doesn't stick. You have to integrate and practice, you have to use this and rehearse this, and in that process celebrate every single tiny win.

We'll talk about celebration and what celebration can look like but I want to say here that it's important you celebrate every single step in a forward direction. Our human nature, our human condition, tends to rehearse everything that goes wrong over and over, and as a result we end up integrating *losing*. What you want to do in coaching is shift that and integrate *winning*. That way you start to get in the habit of winning. And that is what rehearsal is all about, you develop a habit of success. And the more you stack little successes, the more you're going to win, the more successes you're going to have.

7. NEXT STEPS

The seventh step is to actually take the *next* step. I get clients all the time who come to me—and this is exciting because it means we're doing a great job in the coaching—and they say, "I'm not sure what we're going to talk about today—*everything is going so well!* Everything is humming along really fabulously." Now that's good of course, I like that! That is just awesome. But what's important really is that we get into the practice or the habit of asking, "What's the next level?" If you've reached success, if on the wheel of life, you're operating on nines and tens, that becomes your new baseline. It's not horrible—it's good—but you hear people who are in personal development talking about going to the next level. You hear it all the time, whether it's Tony Robbins or Brian Tracy or Tom Hopkins, or John Maxwell, they all talk about going to the next level. In fact every speaker I hear talks about going to the next level.

Well, this is what next level is, when you take all your nines and tens and create *new* nines and tens, bigger and better nines and tens. And you want to always be looking at taking those next steps so that there's momentum in your life.

I've seen so many people, and maybe you've experienced this, where "Gosh, all the wheels are on. Everything's rolling!" They then just coast along and it's really weird—success *stops*. It's because there's no longer that thing they're reaching for. There's not that never-ending improvement, even if it's small tweaks or moving into a new arena or just improving what you're doing. It could be doing it for a different audience or a different type of client, or going a new direction with your company. That expansion, that growth is important.

GROW OR DIE

One of my textbooks in college was called *Grow or Die*. It's interesting, that whole premise. Homeostasis is interesting. Our bodies, for example, are regenerating all of the time. Life cycles and regenerates all of the time. Everything is designed for constant growth, so we want to look at what our next step is.

This concept is a distinction in my coaching framework that is very different from how other coaches proceed. When most others reach that destination, they don't have a next level. Instead it's kind of like, "Now what?" And you're not done. If you've succeeded, that former nine is now the new five and you have to ask what the next level is.

And those are the Seven Keys to coaching. Now we will go into greater detail of each one, chapter by chapter.

KEY 1: CREATE RELATIONSHIP

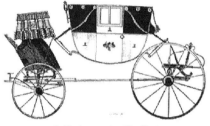

A Neat Ornamented, or Town Coach

Flatter me, and I may not believe you. Criticize me, and I may not like you. Ignore me, and I may not forgive you. Encourage me, and I will not forget you. Love me and I may be forced to love you.

—William Arthur Ward

COACHING IS A PARTNERSHIP with your client. Yet we live in an age of disconnect, where many are starved for or have given up on meaningful connection, and it doesn't have to be this way.

The rise of technology as a social mechanism, the ability to edit our lives, and the expectation of immediate gratification have all contributed to the notion that relationships are found and not made. Yet if there is no relationship there can be no helping your client. If there is no relationship there is seldom satisfaction or fulfillment. The thing that makes you a stranger to someone is simply a lack of relationship. The difference between an effective, happy coach (and client) and an unsuccessful coach is primarily the ability to create relationship.

In fact, we are in relationship with more people and more things than we might realize. Good relationships start with empathy and compassion, and these can in fact be learned. Hospice has an amazing exercise they do in their training to help people understand and create compassion, which follows:

GIVE YOURSELF A GIFT

Do this exercise:

- Get together four different colored sheets of paper. Each color will represent something different. For example:
- Blue: what you value most (love, honor, excitement, and so on)

- Goldenrod: favorite foods

- Green: things you love to do

- Pink: favorite living people you personally know

- Cut each page into five pieces, so you have five pieces of each color.

- Take five pieces of one color, and on that color—on blue for example—write one thing on each piece of paper that you value most; for example, "love," and so on.

- Now pick another color—for example goldenrod—and on these five write five of your favorite foods.

- On another color—green for example—write down five things you love to do.

- On another color—perhaps pink—write down five of your favorite, most important living people in your life—not celebrities or people you've never met, but people actually in your life, your favorite people.

- Now turn them all over so the names are face down. For example, if we start with blue, or the things you value most, turn them over so they're face down and mix them around.

- Now pick one of those pieces, turn it over, and imagine your life without that thing you value most, imagine that you will never have that thing in your life again. Feel what that's like, feel how that is.

- Next turn over a piece of a different color—goldenrod for food, for example—and imagine you can never taste this food again ever in your life.

- Next turn over the color for all those things you love to do (green in this example) and imagine you can never do this again. For example, I love driving. If I could never drive again I would be devastated—I have such a visceral reaction to that.

- Next turn over the pieces of paper with people's names on them (pink in this example). Move them around, mix them up, and select one. Imagine if you could never, ever have this person in your life again.

- And now, because we want everyone to be whole, give yourself the gift of giving that person back to you. Give the gift of that activity back to you. Feel the joy, actually consider what that feels like to have those things and that person restored back into your life. And notice how we have a relationship with food, with activities, with values, and of course with people.

This is a great exercise to develop and to notice relationship, and here's the important thing: Every one of your clients will have a relationship with every one of these things as well. In order to really be in relationship with your client, then, you're going to want to have this level of compassion. Even if you think what they're going through is a tiny thing, they may have a larger association with it, and you want to help them strategize and help them gain whatever skill they need to move forward and to then have what they need in their life.

RAPPORT

rap·port: *a close and harmonious relationship in which the people or groups concerned understand each other's feelings or ideas and communicate well.* —Google definition

Rapport is the kind of relationship you want to have with your client, and integral to establishing rapport is to create a safe space and two-way communication. You want to rapidly get into the use of rapport, and being in it with your client, so it's important to see that relationship building involves two-way communication as well as a safe space where a relationship can prosper.

THE GREETING EXERCISE

Something you can use to check on your level of rapport is what I call the Greeting Exercise. You might want to find someone in your life to test this, or you might just imagine someone there with you as you do this. Imagine that as you meet someone, you shake their hand and greet them, yet you just know they don't care about who you are. Maybe they don't look at you directly or they reach out kind of half-heartedly and have no grip—kind of like a fish-handshake or just weak. Maybe they turn away and they're just completely disconnected. We all know what this feels like—there's no rapport.

And then there's the case where you go to greet someone and they're kind of studying you. They have a look on their face and they're kind of analyzing you with a preconceived notion of "I already don't like you and why am I doing this?" Again, there's no rapport.

Now, on the other hand, let's say you go to greet a long lost friend—somebody you haven't seen in a long, long time. Anyone who's had this happen knows it's all hugs and kisses and love, where you're completely in rapport. It's mutual and you're really in relationship.

ACTIVE LISTENING

There are ways to build rapport. Experimenting or imagining these things as in the Greeting Exercise above should help you realize the differences, for starters. But how do we build rapport, especially if we're coaching? One way is with *active listening*. I've observed that coaching today has moved away from being like therapy, where you're sitting in an office across a table from one another or across the room with the client on the couch. In fact coaching is not usually even done in person anymore. I won't say it's never done like that, but it's mostly not.

Coaching today is done mainly by computer, over an iPad or over the phone. You're normally not in the same room, so how do you develop rapport electronically? Certainly listening becomes very important. And there is what we call *active listening*. It's really important that you stay engaged in what they're saying and don't ever *assume* you've heard what they've said—that's the way to get into deep trouble and to get out of rapport really quickly. You want to check in, to be real. If you're not positive you know what they've said, be real and ask. Don't try to be the sharpest tool in the shed. Don't be Mr. Smarty Pants. You want to ask and be sure that how they said it and how you understood it is *exactly* how they meant it. In active listening you're on the edge of your seat. You are not lackadaisical; you are not on your computer reading emails; you are not texting someone else. You are completely all-in, all-ears, and you will find your rapport level will go way up if you are fully engaged.

You might want to try this exercise, and you might have another coach you can try this with. Really and truly, when I'm teaching this in a room, I have the coaches seated either next to each other or facing each other, and they have a conversation. You ask a question or a series of questions, and when it's over you repeat back the story the other shared to see how accurate you are with it. You let your partner go for three or four minutes and then share back what was said. It can be amazing. We all know the game called "Telephone," wherein one person shares something that gets relayed to the next and the next and the next and twenty people later it's amazing—the final version is nothing like the original message, right? So check in with your client if you need to see how well you are understanding them.

Next I have the coaches stand back to back where they can't see each other. And again, it's amazing. We've become such a visual society since the MTV, VH1 era. People think everything is what you *see*. Well, it's not what you see. In coaching and in life you want to pay attention and you want to be able to develop real rapport. You want to be able to almost hear what's in the gap between what the client says and what happens next, without presuming anything. And you want to check in to see if there's accuracy as needed. It helps create a safe space for coaching.

A safe space is really where the client feels that you are so real and so actively listening to what they are doing that they in fact can express their real thoughts, their real fears, their real desires, and not just give you the party line, not just what sounds good or what they think you want to hear. You want the truth. You want them to be real, and in order for the client to be real you have to be real. You absolutely have to be all-in.

KEEPING IT REAL

I would also say in regard to building rapport, that it is really up to you as the coach to discover what works with your client, and you do want to share a little bit about who you are. For example, I'm a mother. So it might be important for someone who is a mom or a dad with kids to know I've actually raised two kids. I am also dealing with my kids being away now. I've worked through the things my kids didn't do really well coming out of high school, but we did strategize, they did go off and have a life, and they did go back to university and graduate at the tops of their respective classes.

If it might be appropriate for that particular client, this might be important to share.

It can be very important when I'm helping a client build a business, helping them to strategize and build their team, for them to know I had a *horrible* real estate career that I developed into a very *successful* real estate career. So I know how to do it wrong, and I know how to do it right. It might be important to share such a thing with your client so it gives you credibility, so they know you've walked in their moccasins. You want to be real and you want your clients to know you.

But let's be clear: Being real doesn't mean you're going to share your own pains and fears with them. In therapy that's called transference, and it can happen in coaching, too. Always remember that you're working with your client on your client's desires and your client's fulfillment, not yours. If you need to work on getting through your own pains and fears, you need to get a coach! But you do want to be a human being, have emotion, and be engaged. You don't just prescribe—give them an assignment—and that's it. You want to be compassionate and you want to be real and to be human. It's important. Make sense?

MIRRORING AND MATCHING

Regardless of whether you're coaching on the phone or in person—or perhaps you're on Skype, which is actually a little of both—I think it's important that you really understand how some of these rapport techniques work. It's in our nature to build rapport. The famous Neuro-Linguistic Programming (NLP) "grandfathers," Richard Bandler and John Grinder, recognized what we as human beings do by nature and they were able to formulate it into tools that can be replicated and used by anyone. It's like they took the ability from the unconscious competence that we operate out of and they created tools that you can now use, including *mirroring and matching*, which help to build rapport.

Matching is literally when you are doing the same as the other person. If they move their left arm, you use your left arm. That's matching. With mirroring you're likely doing the opposite because you're doing it as if you're looking in a mirror. In mirroring, you might be positioned across from someone and if they use their left arm, you use your right arm. If they are twiddling their left fingers you are twiddling your right fingers, and if they cross their right leg over you cross your left leg over. You don't want to do it obnoxiously. If you do it well they begin to feel very comfortable because you are in rapport. It's amazing.

You should understand you can knock yourself out of rapport, however. If your tonality, the pace of your speech, or the volume of your voice are too different than that of your client, even though you're doing these mirroring things, you can knock yourself totally out of rapport with him or her. That's important to know because mirroring and matching can happen through the voice and on the phone.

For example, in matching, if my client is talking super fast and he's pushing to do things and he's just going, going, going, I'm going to speed up how I'm talking with him. By the same token, if my client is very methodical in how she's speaking and her tone is down lower, I'll go lower. I may not go as low as my client but I am going to match the client enough so they feel that I get them. I am in rapport with them. You want to match the volume, the tone, and the pace of how they're speaking. Sometimes you'll match their accent, too, possibly by accident (or perhaps it's just how I am). I have lots of Australian clients, for example, and we all speak English but you'll find we all start having accents because our innate desire is to be in rapport with each other. It can be comical.

You might find it powerful to actually try out the matching and mirroring. They both work. Practice with another coach or a friend and practice in person. But the key in coaching is to practice with your voice. Practice being in harmony, in rapport. *Rapport is about being in harmony with your client.* You know when you're in harmony and you know when there's discord. Using your voice and getting in tune with your client is very important. I would practice it, especially if you've not done much of it. I would be practicing, practicing, practicing.

POWERFUL QUESTIONS

Another way to develop rapport is to ask powerful questions. (We're going to talk more about asking questions when we get into the *rewiring and resetting* sections of the book, but we're now still in the *explore and examine* steps of coaching.) Your questions should demonstrate that you are interested, that you are engaged. They need to be pertinent to your client's current situation and also pertinent to where the client wants to go and what they want to make happen.

Asking a client "why" generally leads you into therapy, so I prefer asking questions more along these lines:

"Well, what would have to happen for you to achieve that?"

"How would it look"

"How would it feel if you had that result or if you were in that?"

"How would you like it to be instead?"

Asking questions that start with "what" and "how" and "where" are far more powerful than trying to get analytical with "why." After all, what's the answer to "why?" I mean, it's the never ending black hole, right? That's not to say we never use the question "why"—there are moments in which it is pertinent—but in general it's not where I start.

PARTNERSHIP & HARMONY

Again, coaching is a partnership with your client. You are going to move forward and into the future together, and you want it to be safe. We'll speak to creating a safe space more in a moment, but certainly one thing that has to be there is to have that rapport with the client. If there is no relationship with someone in putting something forward, it simply doesn't work. You're not going to share fully. You won't "get" each other. You have to be in a safe space of two-way communication.

Remember that your coaching is a partnership, and that rapport is all about harmony. With these basics established, you can proceed to find out who your client really is, what's running them and what their needs are, and get into the business of really making a difference in their lives and businesses.

KEY 2: EXPLORE

A New Ornamented, or Town Coach

IN THE OVERVIEW OF the Seven Keys of Coaching, the first keys are the "Explore and Examine" Keys. They are followed by the rewiring and resetting Keys. A lot of time in coaching, and a lot of depth to it, goes into exploring and examining who the person is, how they are wired, and why they are doing what they are doing, as well as what habits they have and what values they have, what beliefs they have and all those pieces. And after you've created a relationship and there is true rapport where, as we say in the internet business, you do business with people you know, like, and trust, so that whole first key is creating relationship. This is all about building relationship so that client knows, likes and trusts you as a coach.

The Second Key is to really explore who they are and how they are wired, why they do what they do and why they make the choices they do.

THE HIDDEN CAUSE OF STRESS

Many people have different ways they handle stresses in the different areas of their lives, areas such as career, finances, relationships, family and health. What's fascinating is that a person can be wired to function particularly brilliantly in one area of their life, based on their beliefs and values. For example, your client's career might be skyrocketing and going fantastic—they've got systems in place and habits that are causing things to operate (because there is cause and effect) really well and to get the results that they want, while all the wheels are off in their relationship because the habits they have and the values they have are at odds with each other. Another example is the type of person I have coached whose relationships are stellar. They have amazing relationships with their kids, with their spouse, with their parents. And at work they are a team player, they have respect from the players and the boss, or they are the boss and the team can't do enough for them. But all the wheels are off in terms of money and in terms of production, and really getting where they want to go. On the other hand, many executives have their careers working perfectly, and good, satisfying relationships, but their health—I mean seriously, they are a heart attack waiting to happen.

Now I'm talking about succeeding in all of these different areas. There are cases in which a person's career is rewarding, but the finances suck, or you've got a career that is going really well but with the relationship all the wheels are falling off. I've got a client whose health is spectacular, they are fit, they're healthy and they are going to live to 105 and they are doing well but they can't get anything going in the area of their career. So really, truly, we all have different areas of our lives that we are best at, but the trick to real fulfillment is to have all of the plates spinning. Being able to keep them all in the air without being caught in frenetic energy is done by ensuring that you have values and beliefs that are congruent with one another -- that you don't have one set of rules for life in one area and a conflicting set of rules, habits, values or beliefs in another.

What happens so often is we are living unconsciously. Most people, the average public person, is not asking himself, "Oh, gee, what are my habits in my career? What are my habits in the area of finance? What are my habits in the area of my relationships? And what are my values in all of these areas of all of my life? What beliefs do I have in every single one of those areas?" Well, here's the thing: What if they clash? What if they are not congruent? A good example is, "You know what, I spend the money I have because I want to live in the present; and as to my relationships, I believe I should be with these people I care about, should make time with the people I love in the here and now; and I also believe that I ought to be at work and go the extra mile and spend that extra couple of hours every day—that if you work hard you're going to be successful."

So notice, you can't be in all places at all times. So these things are in conflict and what you find is that the conflicts cause enormous unconscious stress. You don't even know why you're stressed, but you feel frenetic, or you feel depressed, or you feel overwhelmed, or you feel any number of emotions, and in those moments it's like you can't quite get all the plates in the air, spinning.

THE WHEELS OF LIFE AND BUSINESS

One very traditional thought—and this is something I learned from Zig Ziglar back in the 1970s, so it's certainly not an original thought—is the whole concept of a life wheel, what we call the wheel of life (since those days we also have a wheel of business) because you want to look at what areas all the areas are that are taking your client's attention or that need their attention, and how are they doing? And everybody has their own different wheel of life so this example is only that—an example. I love using the six F's, at least to get people started:

- There's Fun: all the play time and the leisure and the travel;

- There's Family: your relationships, the kids and the parents, the spouse, and the team at work and all of that;

- Then there's Factory: so that's your career and what you're doing, as well as how you make your money;

- There's Finances: what you do with your money;

- There is Fitness, your health area;

- And there's Faith, of course. We have a spiritual life, whether it's a formal church or temple that you prescribe to or it's just meditation, taking time out, enjoying nature, or whatever your form of faith is, we are spiritual beings. Peace, calm and centeredness are very often disrupted when we don't have that area of our lives, in some form, attended to.

It's important to look at that. An example of a business wheel or a wheel of business would look at the areas in your business. Now everybody has a different business, but a sample would be you've got employees, or you've got the boss, or you've got the team of people and there's that aspect. There are the systems at work. There's the admin at work. There are the sales at work. There is the marketing at work and maybe nowadays you have to look at social media for exposure. There is the IT department nowadays and obviously each of these areas could be a wheel of its own. If you are in charge of the IT department there would be all the different wedges of the pie, as it were, on the wheel that would be part of that.

And then what I ask people to do—let's just take the wheel of life, for example—is to go around and use a rating system of "0" to mean it could not get any worse and "10" couldn't get any better. I have them take each of those wedges or pieces of the pie or wheel and go around and score from 0 to 10: How are your finances? Meaning how is it with what you're doing with your money, your investments, how are your growing your money, your budget, your debt, that sort of thing, 0 to 10. How is your family? How are your relationships doing? I often have people divide that wedge into three-part portions. If they have children I have children on one wedge, if they have a spouse I have that as another wedge, and then I have another one for extended family and friends, and they score that from 0 to 10.

I go along and really look to see where people are in their life. This is really just exploring, now. You are seeing, how is their life? Before you go into working on it get a baseline to see what they're doing. It's always fascinating for them to color in their wheel. Their fitness might be a 9, and their career might be a 6, and their relationships might be a 2, their faith might be a 3. And then you have them color it in and you ask, "Okay, how do you think the vehicle called life is going to be running on a wheel that looks like this?" Of course it never fails because it looks ridiculous.

Now I've had clients who pretty much have an average life. Their wheel is not splayed out like I just described, instead it is all 4s and 5s. So yes, it's going to roll evenly, but it's not on an inflated tire. It's not rolling at its full potential. I will say, if you know anything about tires, if they are running on less air than they are required to have they wear out very quickly and tear, and you wear the edges out. A little bit of a metaphor for people in their lives.

HUMAN NEEDS

The goal of coaching, of course, is for people to have fulfillment and have rich, full lives that are full of all of the things that are important to them. So I'm certainly not going to put on everyone that they've got to be gym rats or that they need to be marathon runners. I'm not going to put on everyone that they've got to be multibillionaires. I'm not going to put on everyone that they have got to run a huge Fortune 500 company. But for them, what is a 10? So we will look at that in a moment, not quite yet. For now we are going to leave it be. But as we get into coaching and into transformation (which is Key 4) we will then assess what the wheel is doing. We will assess what a 10 would look like. We will start to really work on, "How do we want it to be instead?" Right now we are just exploring what is.

Robert Schindler, Abraham Maslow, and Tony Robbins have all done work—extreme work, notorious work—on human needs. They've called it "hierarchy of needs," called it "man's needs"—they all have different names for this. Robbins calls it "six human needs." I'm going to utilize that particular model because it's the most recent version that I've seen, but here's the thing: I don't care which psychologist that you go with, which school of psychology you run with, the premise is that every human on the planet has the same needs. When you're talking to a client, you don't need to wonder what their needs are, because they need the following basic things. And so without going into huge depth, I will just say the four basic survival needs are:

- Security or Certainty, depending on which school of thought you go with.
- Variety or Uncertainty. Or in other words, every human being has the need for some surprise, for some variance. Why in the world do we have a million restaurants? Because nobody wants to eat the same thing every single day for the rest of their lives. Why do affairs happen? Because after 30 years or 20 years or 10 years it's like, "I need a little variety!" But I will say that if you know this you can create this within the confines of where you are living.
- Importance or Significance. Man has the need to matter.
- Love and Connection. Man is wired to be part of community. There's scripture, there are proverbs, there are amazing sayings by wise men and women that always lead to how we need to be connected with one another. The more the more recent term is, "It takes a village."

I will just go out on a limb here and say for all of these needs we have mature, grown-up, evolved ways of demonstrating and having them show up and living them out in our lives. We all also have ways of doing them inappropriately, immaturely, and completely harmfully for ourselves and others. It's absolutely where coaching needs to help, where coaching does in fact help.

Now if you are meeting all four of those needs there are also fulfillment needs. Man has a need to be fulfilled and that's where growth, learning, education, expanding, being more, overcoming challenges, creating more, contributing, where that drive for growth in man is huge. The need to contribute is in fact the reason coaching came into the being. I believe it's the reason that psychology came into being back when. People wanted to make a difference. People wanted to help other people. If you look at nursing and doctoring, besides the fact that we want to be well and we want to live and not die, there are a lot of people who are just called to want to help people. It's the reason we've got foundations. It's the reason we've got people going around the world when there's a big earthquake and whole cities and communities are crashed and we've got people flying all over the world to help them. That need to contribute, to make a difference, to help, is how we're wired as human beings.

I have to also say that if you have no security or certainty, or you have no love and connection, or you have no feeling of importance, if these basic survival pieces aren't being met on any level, let me tell you, there's no way you're going to go save somebody. There is no way that you care about growth because you're in a survival mode.

Those are the needs, and here's the thing: the requirement to meet those needs in our life is the driving force. Now, we're meeting those needs, but *how* are we meeting those needs? We have beliefs (that we learn more about in the Five Star Formula) and we have values that actually are layered underneath meeting those needs. Everybody meets those needs differently. We're driven to meet our needs but how we are driven to meet those needs is through our beliefs and through our values.

HIERARCHY OF VALUES

So let me start with values. What's a value? How do you know what your values are? One of the key questions you can ask if you want to know what you value is: What's most important to you in life? That's a value. And then I would say in the areas of your life: What's important to you in your health? What's important to you in your relationship? What's important to you about parenting and raising kids? Those pieces determine your values. They're going to tell you which values you have, like, "Well, what's important to me in life? It's important for me to take care of my family. For me it's important to be a responsible, contributing citizen. Those are what I value. What's important to me is being educated and using my education, actually using the brains I have—that's important to me. I value that. I think it's important to work on being healthy and pay attention to what I eat and exercise. That's important to me, so I value that."

Now here's where it gets really interesting. So let's just say you've determined your values. What if on one hand you think, "It's really important to be early to work and to work like a mad dog and to really hit it out of the park and to really make every last call and I value getting the job done in a day even if it takes me 14 hours. And yet I value spending time with my children and I value being home with my spouse for dinner and I think that's important. And I also value that it's important to work out every single day and you really do a full workout where you've got a program and you do cardio and weights and all of that."

Now, can you hear what's going on? Values are starting to conflict. One of the very critical things in coaching is to be aware of what people value because you start to see where they could have some conflicts and where they might need to look at them and make conscious decisions. Living consciously is so critical to getting things done and having a fulfilling, satisfying life.

Then it's important to really look at prioritizing these values. What I value might move around from day to day and might exchange places so that is totally possible. On any given day if I have not worked out for a day or two because I had other choices I made, then my priorities might move around. But in general you want to look at your whole list of what you value and you might want to then prioritize and decide what your hierarchy of those values are:

"Is A more important than B?"

"No, B is more important!"

"Alright, then is B more important than C?"

"No, C is more important!"

"Well, is C more important than B?"

"Yes."

So we put the hierarchy in order. Then after we determine that, here is a tricky piece. You actually discover that there are rules to meet the value. If "love" is a high value to me and if "work" is a high value, here's what happens that's very interesting and it's so important for coaches to understand, or for that matter, for managers or human resource people who want to understand their employees. It's so critical to understand, that they value work, and everyone has rules. I will just come out and say this: Every disagreement between two people, whether they are a married couple or a parent and a child, or just two friends, every disagreement is a *rules* disagreement. I can't tell you how many times I've coached couples or coached business partners and they are just at each others' throats about something and they both appear to place the same value on. For example, business partners might both want to get the same contract for this big job, but they both have a different rule about how they're going to make that happen, about what has to happen in order to get that.

One partner begins with, "I believe that we have to go flying off to Singapore and have meetings with people."

And the other one believes, "We need to take care of our families first and we can do that all over Skype."

People have different rules about how to make things happen. It's important to look at everything you value this way: ask the question, "What has to happen in order for me to experience that value, for me to have that value? For that value to show up in my life, what has to happen?" That's where you're defining what the rule is about that value. I coached a middle-aged couple who both had "love" at the top of their list. They both had "family" second on their list. So you would think they were in complete agreement.

Here I asked the question, "Well, for love to happen, what has to happen for you to experience love in this relationship?"

And she said, "The two of us go off on vacation on a regular basis. We have dinner every night together. We spend time occasionally with the kids and with our families." That was her definition.

His answer, when I asked the question, was, "Oh my gosh. The kids come over every night with dinner. I spend time going on holidays with my kids. I spend time occasionally going on holidays with my wife..." But you can see the disconnect. Totally different rules and priorities. That's where exploring and discovering where conflict exists emotionally in their lives shows up really easily with these questions.

And then, what do they believe? In all these areas of their lives you go around the wheel and ask, "What's true about your fitness? What do you believe about your fitness?" What's going to show up is what's important. What's going to show up is what their truth is in their life, and again, you're going to notice that there might be conflict. If there is conflict you are going to need to work through that in transformation and make choices and decisions, but again, this is about living consciously. Once you determine what their wheel of business and their wheel of life are, and you have them score those areas, you're going to go around and find out what their needs are, but you want to discover which of those needs are driving them first and foremost. You are going to also want to know which of these areas on these wheels are most important to them and what they believe about each one of these areas. This is going to give you an incredible platform. Once you've done that you are going to look at where the obvious conflicts are, where there is going to be friction. Or as I like to put it, are they talking out of both sides of their mouths? Are they saying, "Gee, working and making all this money, that's most of my time there, that's most important—Oh no, having children! Raising the children! Being home with the children—that's most important!" A little conflict there, a very obvious one. They are sometimes much more subtle than that but those are really important pieces.

HELP YOUR CLIENT CREATE THE IDENTITY THEY WANT

I need to quote Tony Robbins on this because in my 24 years of coaching I've found this to be true. He says that the most important piece of the human personality is the need to remain consistent with who you say you are. That is code for, "You are going to do whatever it takes to remain consistent with your identity." Who you say you are, your identity, is the most pivotal piece of any of this, and here's why: If you remove your identity, you're lost. You don't really know who you are or what you are and it's the reason there are crises when someone loses their job. They get shown the door and they no longer have that career that they worked so hard to get. It is so prevalent with, typically, women who become empty-nesters. It's like their whole identity was raising those kids—and they've spent all their time raising those kids. It's like their identity was being a mother, and now they're not. Or their identity was being a CEO of a Fortune 500 company and now they're not. So if they're not and they haven't made a plan to shift their identity, they're lost.

An identity is who you say you are, and who you say you're not. At any time the way to find someone's identity is by asking them about themselves: "I'm good at... I'm short. I'm skinny. I'm horrible at..." And what they say they're not is equally as defining: "I'm terrible at math. I'm great at writing. I'm horrible at navigating. I'm great at driving." Those are all parts of your identity. Those are all defining pieces. You hear your friends (and yourself, if you're honest) say these things all of the time. This is all code for your identity: who you say you are and who you say you are not.

Here's the good news: We were not born with it. You actually, along the road and unconsciously, created your identity. Most of us created our identity out of our parents telling us what we are good and bad at, what our friends then told us we were great and bad at (and boy did they ever), what our teachers and all of your key people and players we respected and believed in our lives told us we were great or bad at. In my case it was my parents, a couple of friends of my parents that I really loved and respected and believed, and my husband at the time, who all told me how great I would be, how awesome I was at sales. "You would be awesome at real estate!" So of course, I went out and did real estate. And they were right! I was fantastic at it, except I never asked myself if that was the identity that I wanted. But it's what I did for 18 years, even though I hated it. "Hate" might be too strong a word, but it was not my favorite thing at all and I was excited when I made choices and actually realized that my identity was different than being a real estate salesperson. And here's the good news today:

Your client can choose to have whatever identity they decide that they want.

And all I tell people is to write down the words "I am." I am what? "I am fit. I am lean. I'm smart. I'm intelligent." Pick the words and characteristics you want. So here's the question that goes with that: What characteristics must you demonstrate on a daily basis in order for you to be—and you can fill in the blank—to be successful? To be a career person? To be an entrepreneur? To be healthy and fit? To be a fantastic wife or husband? To be a great parent? And then just answer the question and keep answering it. I came up with about 60 words and then eliminated some that were synonymous, and came up with a beautiful list of who I decided I wanted to be. The only thing you have to do to change your identity—because all you've done all these past many years is rehearse in your head that you were that person, that thing, that description—is rehearse the description you choose and rehearse it again and again and again until it's integrated inside of you. And here's the shocker: They say it takes 21 days to create a habit, right? I like to say you can take it for 45 days to actually cement that in and have it show up. I'll tell you, 45 days into this and you will have people saying your words back to you. If one of your words was "focused," people will say to you, "You are so focused!" If some of your words, as they were in my case, were "effective and efficient," people are going to say to you—and they did say to me—"You're so effective and efficient!" Oh my gosh, when the words started coming back to me I was stunned and amazed, and I was a believer.

It's just so important to really look at the identity of this client you're talking with. Who do they say they are and who do they say they're not? And as you explore and then you assess, you then can determine what part of this—we don't throw the baby out with the bathwater—but what parts of this do you want to transform? What pieces do you want to keep? Where are there conflicts? Between the needs, the values, the beliefs and their identity, where are they rubbing each other the wrong way? Where are they trying to go north and south at the same time? If you do nothing more in your coaching, in your helping your employees or your clients or patients with just this illumination, this will change a life. When they get out of their conflicts there is such a calm and a centered peace in someone because everything is going the same direction. All of a sudden, it's very easy to hit targets and accomplish what they want to accomplish, really easy to make things happen.

SUB-MODALITIES AND FILTERS

In Neuro Linguistic Programming (NLP) there is a term called "sub modalities." It means "filters," or how we filter life. An example of this is noting how my clients sort things. Do they sort by noting that, "Everything is the same except that piece over there is different," or do they notice that "Everything is different than that piece because of x y and z," or do they notice "They're different and those two happen to be the same"? It's really interesting. I happen to be somebody who sorts by sameness. In fact last year I discovered something about myself. I kept wondering, why do I always chime in and say, "Oh, I did that too?" It was annoying people, to be honest, because it was like I was always trying to one-up them. But when analyzed it, I found I sort by sameness. And because I notice what's the same, I'm always noticing how I do it the same. That's the motive behind it. I want to notice this in my clients because when I communicate with them I want to take into account whether they sort by sameness. There's also another feature that is related in filtering: people mismatch or they try to match. I'm a matcher, I like matching people. I like being like people so I try to say what's the same: "Oh yes, me too!" But there are people who are mis-matchers who are going to say the opposite, no matter what you say. If you know that about them you're going to communicate in a way that they actually can hear you and there's not strife in the conversation. It's not that we're trying to change them. It's that we want to work with who they are.

Now this is not a book about NLP so I'm not going to dive deep into this conversation, but I do want to make people aware that these sub modalities are important to know so that you know who it is that's in front of you and who you're communicating with, who you're working with, who you are living with.

Another key filter, in this same topic, is—and this is really important in coaching—are they moving toward something are they moving away from it? So when you get to target planning and really executing and implementing in Key 5, you will already know whether you need lots of leverage because they are likely to move away from something, or whether to build the case for moving towards something. I can use real estate as a great example of this (I realize now, after having sold houses for years and years, this was a concept I had been innately applying. Had I known, I would very much still use it today). I had clients moving to Utah from sunny Southern California where there's 22 million people. They were moving *away*, getting out of the smog, getting out of the congestion and getting away from the traffic. That's an example of (literally) moving away. And I had some clients who'd say, "I'm going to Colorado! I can't wait to go to the mountains! I can't wait to have fresh air! I can't wait to have that beautiful sky at night!" They were more motivated by moving *towards* something than moving away from it. So you want to listen to your clients to understand if they are being pulled towards a goal. Do they really want the prize, or are they moving away from something? Are they sick and tired of driving a crappy car, living in a horrible house, and being in a horrible neighborhood? You need to ask yourself if they are moving toward or away. These are all important filters. This is all such critical information to know about someone so that you can really move into assessing all the parts of their life and going in and transforming what's happening with them.

THE PSYCLE OF PERFORMANCE

Now we're going to go into the "Psychle of Performance." I spell "cycle" in this case as "psychle." That's where we are really going dive down. Everyone has a Psychle of Performance and we will explore where they are in the Psychle of Performance in each of the areas of their life. You're going to find that some people will be in excitement in their relationships and they're going to be in disillusionment with work, or they're going to be in a breakthrough in the area of their health. It's going to vary. And how they handle disillusionment can help them break through every time. If they're aware and conscious of how to do it, it's going to be very powerful, so we'll go into depth on that.

There are four phases in the Psychle of Performance, and important things to understand. When you start a new job, a new relationship, a new project or even a new sport, you are about to go through four distinct phases. The key to finishing well is to know how to go through these four phases so you go completely through them and you go through them well, and you do actually go through to the next level. It is a bona fide cycle of performance because it is a mental circle. You go through the cycle over and over and over again at different times in your experience.

I'll use my parents' relationship as an example. They were married over 63 years. I can tell you, I watched them— now that I'm conscious to this—go through these four cycles over and over until they went to the next level, then the next level, and the next level until they finished their lives and died just nine weeks apart.

PHASE 1: EXCITEMENT

Anytime you start something—for example, a coach starting a new practice or anyone embarking on a new project of any kind—in any beginning, we tend to fall in love and be enthralled with the new job, project, or relationship at first.

So the first phase is the excitement phase. I'll use a relationship as an example but you can think about this in terms of a job, a sport, an activity you like—it doesn't matter. Just remember that when you first start a relationship, you fall passionately in love, you can't be without that other person, you are tied at the hip. You start a conversation on the phone (you may have had this experience), and by 3 A.M. in the morning you're still talking, on and on and on. Never running out of things to say, never running out of laughter, sharing new ideas, you are in the excitement phase. It is *magnificent*— you can't imagine life in any other way, right?

PHASE 2: DISILLUSIONMENT

Then we hit the stage called "disillusionment." Whether it's a job or whether it's an activity or a relationship, we go through this phase. I'm starting to watch my daughter as a new mother herself start the disillusionment phase! Up until this point, she's been so excited about this new baby! And remember, with the new relationship, all of a sudden, all the quirky little things this person does, or all the endless, daily-ness of being a new mother, you go into this disillusionment phase because you start realizing, "Gee, this isn't very much fun," or "I don't really like that they talk when their mouth is full," or "I don't like that they're not making progress in their new business," if you're a wife or even a coach. "Where are all the results? What's happening with that?" All the wonderfulness starts to get a little dull or a little tarnished. We've all been there. I'll cover the different ways you might go through the disillusionment, but I'll finish summing up the psychle phases here first.

PHASE 3: BREAKTHROUGH

The third phase is breakthrough. When in relationships or on a job, or in parenthood, you find a way to break through. You find a way to tackle the problem differently. You find strategies. You find tools, you develop skills so that you can get through and work around the disillusionment—because understand, the disillusionment is on *your* part; it's *your* perception that is causing disillusionment and it is on you, not the other person, not the boss, not the baby, not your partner to shift and change. It's for you to do. And this is where coaching is all about identifying how you go through disillusionment. It's not a matter of whether you're going to have disillusionment, you simply will get into disillusionment in life, and in every facet of life. So it's really about what you do with it. Do you develop skills? Do you find tools? Do you get different strategies? Do you start to view it differently? Do you get a different perspective? And a coach can help you to break through and develop all of those things so you do break through.

The breakthrough phase is not a long phase. It's a phase where you adopt new perspectives, new tools and skills, new views, and then you go to the fourth phase.

PHASE 4: TRANSFORMATION AND IDENTITY

The fourth phase is transformation and identity. You have a different way of being, a different way of tackling disillusionment. You break through, you transform and you become different in the way that you actually do the job, or you get the results. Or maybe it's that you are in a relationship and the way that you participate in the relationship or in the way that you parent the child, or the way you do the activity or the sport or the hobby.

So what's important is that you realize all four of these phases are pertinent and the minute you get to transformation you've arrived and things get exciting again. You get a new excitement about being a parent, for example. You're at a new phase of this child's childhood or a new phase of this relationship that you're in. You're at a new phase and stage of that and there's a new cycle starting. *Notice* that there's a new cycle and a new phase starting again, and the excitement will last until there's something that tarnishes it, and you begin the psychle all over again. Of course this is something that's powerful to understand.

FOUR LEVELS OF COMPETENCE

The Four "Psychles" align perfectly with the Four Levels of Competence, a notion that has been around a long time and is published in many books8. There are four levels of consciousness as it were in the four phases of the Psychle of Performance.

LEVEL 1: UNCONSCIOUS INCOMPETENCE

You'll notice in the excitement phase you are actually *unconsciously incompetent,* because you don't know what you don't know. You hear about these levels often and they apply in the Psychle of Performance. In the excitement phase for example, you don't know the new boyfriend is going to chew his food with his mouth open all the time. You don't know that he's a dreamer and he has no action plan and never has the rubber meet the road. You don't know that the baby—oh my gosh—he's going to do nothing but sleep and poop and

---

[8] Initially described as "Four Stages for Learning Any New Skill", the theory was developed at Gordon Training International by its employee Noel Burch in the 1970s.
(https://en.wikipedia.org/wiki/Four_stages_of_competence)

eat, that's all he's going to do! You have this big dream, right? And you don't realize that on the new job, my gosh, the boss is going to be so demanding, and it never fails—four o'clock on Friday, there are 49 other things to do. You don't know what you don't know.

LEVEL 2: CONSCIOUS INCOMPETENCE

In the disillusionment phase you realize the guy chews with his mouth full. You become *consciously incompetent*, because you become aware of these follies. You become aware that it's going to bother you. You become aware that you don't like it, that it's not really perfect, that gosh, this baby's not going to take care of itself, that I have to be here forever and I'm never going to get a break and it feels like I'm never going to sleep again. It's like, "Oh my gosh, this partner of mine, they're not really doing things the way I think they should." So you become conscious to that, but don't yet know what to do about it to be effective. So you say the wrong thing. You cry. You yell and scream. You have go-to's that are not effective and you're incompetent to make change.

Now what it really is, is that you simply have bad habits there. You become aware of things just enough to realize you don't know what to do with it and you're frustrated.

103

LEVEL 3: CONSCIOUS COMPETENCE

In the third phase of the Psychle of Performance, breakthrough, you become *consciously competent*. This is where you know that you need to change. In fact this is where you actually and on-purpose build a new habit. You get skills, you go get tools, you get strategies, but you're not *unconscious* to them, you've got to pay attention to them. When you first build a new habit it's tedious. You have to be on-purpose every single day. For example, if you want to get fit and you want to be lean and mean and all of that, you have to on-purpose book a trainer at the gym. You have to be at the gym every single day at a certain time. You have to make it to your yoga class and Pilates class. You have to do it *consciously* every single day, on-purpose. Sometimes it takes an act of Congress to get you to go do those things every day because you're building a new habit.

Being consciously competent means that you are consciously aware of what you're doing. You're consciously building a new habit. You're consciously building a strategy, and that's going to cause *breakthrough*. You're breaking through the old and you're going to do it differently and develop a new perspective.

LEVEL 4: UNCONSCIOUS COMPETENT

The fourth phase of being in the Psychle of Performance is being *unconsciously competent.* And that is the same as transformation, it's developing a new way of being, a new way of doing things, but now you don't have to think about it.

You've done all that work in the breakthrough phase, where you had to be consciously competent, consciously building a new habit, and now you've broken through. You've transformed and broken through with the new habit, a new habit you no longer have to think about. I have things—we all do—that I no longer have to think about. I go out every day for my daily hike of three miles and it's just a habit. I just put on my joggers and I'm out doing it, no matter what, every single day. It's like brushing my teeth. I wouldn't think of going out without brushing my teeth. It's just part of the program, it's part of what I'm doing.

So that's the Psychle of Performance and the Four Levels of Competence. The key is getting through the toughest place, which is disillusionment. All the growth happens in disillusionment, when you are consciously incompetent. All the failure, believe it or not, also happens in the disillusionment phase.

Categories of Disillusionment

There are seven categories of disillusionment. Your client won't normally go through all of these but you might find they go through a combination of them, or they might operate in just one way. These are seven loser strategies "for survival" and none of them work.

1. The Victim

The Victim's whole modus operandi is to place blame. They blame the other person, the baby, the job, the company, and so on. Blame, blame, blame, and no participation in getting things running. No ownership. "They" have to fix it. "They" have to make it better. "They" have to approve my life.

2. The Quitter

I find that a lot of addicts, whether their addiction is to alcohol or anything else, fall in this category. They just leave. They go hide out with whatever their addiction is. They hide out at the bar before they go home, or they don't go home at all. They go to their buddy's house and they bail on their marriage, they bail on their kids, they bail on their job. And here's the thing: if they don't figure out new tools and strategies, they may take this manner of going through disillusionment. The quitter just quits, then they go right back into the excitement phase with somebody or something else, and when they get into disillusionment they go right back to quitting again without ever making any progress.

3. THE WIZARD OF OZ

Some people have a mindset that "It's always better over the rainbow." For example, "I've been a real estate agent and it's not working so I'll go into nursing." I had a client who always had some new job she was going into. She was always going to go get some education because it would be better "over there," better were she a nurse, or "No—I'm going into chiropractic now." One time she found a multi-level marketing company she was going into. The fact is *she* is the common denominator that moves from this to this to this and always goes through this phase the same way and is never happy.

4. THE WORRY WART

The Worry Wart's whole life is motivated by doubt, fear, or worry. They start a new job, a new relationship or activity and they are always worried about the liability, about getting hurt and so on, so they don't live life! Hypochondriacs fall into this category. They start, get their toes wet, and then they retract because, "Oh my gosh, something might happen! I might get hurt!" But life is a risk! Let's jump, let's go!

5. THE RUNAWAY

The Runaway is always running off to join the circus somewhere else. They're going off to the ashram over in India because then they don't have to deal with any of their problems. That's the Runaway, they're escape artists.

6. THE ACTOR

Another losing strategy some use to unsuccessfully handle disillusionment is "I'm going to pretend everything is perfect." My favorite example of this on the *Desperate Housewives* TV series. There was a character named Bree Van de Kamp, who looked like she had a perfect life, but we as the audience knew everything was falling apart for her—her marriage was on the rocks, the kids were flunking out of school, and so on. The Actors are your neighbors who live in the perfect house with the white picket fence, with the perfect shutters, all perfectly painted, the roses are manicured, it's all perfect, perfect, perfect. She's the welcome wagon when somebody moves in to the neighborhood and brings you the basket of muffins. Then one day the house is foreclosed on, the husband runs off with the secretary and the kids are in juvenile detention. Their whole life is pretense. They're doing nothing but wearing a mask and pretending, not actually meeting the world where it is, not actually meeting challenges. They're pretending, sweeping it all under the carpet, and it's "all perfect." They do tend to be perfectionists.

7. THE BULL IN THE CHINA SHOP

The Bull in the China Shop is like the character of Scrooge in *A Christmas Carol*. They are going to maul over everyone to get to the top. They are going to climb that ladder at everyone else's expense. They set a goal and get to the top but they leave a wake of carnage behind them. They have no fulfillment, no friends, and may be at "the top" but they've done it at the expense of their marriage, of the relationship with their children, and at the expense of literally having any kind of love or fulfillment in their life.

COACHES NEED COACHES, TOO!

Those are the categories. What's important is that you recognize that the Psychle of Performance is going on in every aspect of your, and your client's, lives. If they have a wheel of life and they have finances, there's family and relationships, there's career and health and fitness, and if you look at all the pieces of the pie in their life, each one is in a phase of the Psychle of Performance. They may be in the excitement phase in one area of their life and they may be in total disillusionment in another, and they may actually be breaking through or transforming in other parts of their life. So it's possible to be at different places at different parts of life, but you need to recognize how they handle disillusionment.

What's your pattern? What is your way of innately doing *conscious incompetent?* In most cases, get a coach! Get a coach to help you develop skills and tools and strategies that are effective, that win, that are fulfilling, in order for you to break through. You've got to solve that destructive pattern.

I had a client who was a sex addict who often went to pornography. They were in complete denial. Well, sometimes it's a matter of getting help to break the addiction. Sometimes it's realizing, "Okay, *I am the common denominator here.* I need to shift my beliefs and my values, and then shift my identity in order to really break through instead of quitting or running away, or instead of being the bull in the china shop, shoving everybody away to get to the top, to get to the destination.

I have lots of tools in this book that can help you help clients develop their new identities, values, beliefs and target plans to create positive futures. It's not a matter of *whether* they go through the Psychle of Performance, it's rather *how they choose to do it*. Doing it with great tools and strategies can help them to become, ultimately, consciously competent and then unconsciously competent where those new habits are the way they operate.

And everyone wins.

KEY 3: ASSESS PERSONALITIES

A Neat Ornamented, or Town Coach

A CLIENT AND A COACH need to assess why the client is making *choices* because those choices create *habits*. There is such a thing as cause and effect, and if the client's current results in life are not what's desired, it's important that you have a look at why. Assessments can be a really useful tool. They help you dig in quickly to figure out what's going on, figure out why things are happening.

I'm going to start by explaining why we use assessments and it's really important to note that this is not about grading a person or about casting where there is right or wrong, it's just *assessing*. We assess different things because we want people to actually realize why they do what they do, identify what habits they've got, and to see what habits they have created that cause them to make the choices that they do. And it's all really about those choices. Sometimes people have habits which they've created, which might have served them at one point, but it's like they don't even know why they have those habits anymore. There's a famous story about a daughter who cuts the ends off of the ham and throws them away. Somebody asks her why she does that and she says, "Gee, my mom always did." So she asked her mom about this, who asked her grandmother, who said back in the old days, the whole ham wouldn't fit in their small oven! The truth is we are all doing stuff like that. But we can assess, and we can even get rid of old habits and create better ones.

So assessments can really help enlighten people about why they are making the choices they are. Then you can choose if they need to change those decisions or if they want to mitigate them—and it certainly is important since all of us are in what I call *relatedness* with everybody on the planet here. It helps us to understand what those people's choices are and maybe why they're making those choices. So this chapter is really about exposing different kinds of personalities, different areas, where you might want to have clients (or you, yourself) do an assessment, just to kind of check in with yourself or to check in with your client to know where they're coming from.

Keep in mind these are *assessments* and they're not *tests*. There are no right answers—it's simply *information*. That's why as a coach I think assessments are so powerful. They give you insight into who your client is, and assessing immediately gives you some help to be able to move ahead with them.

A PERSONAL STORY

On a personal note, at one time I did have a husband leave, then a week later my dad died. Nine weeks after that my mother died. I had just moved and then suddenly had to move again within six months—which meant a job change, because, as someone who worked with a local client base, I now had to build up a new one. I also had to do all of this estate stuff with my sisters and we were not in agreement. One sister wanted one thing, the other sister wanted another, and I wanted something totally different. It was very, very, challenging. Meanwhile my son was trying to get into college and my daughter decided she was going to have a baby. There was stress on every level. I just about had *red line* stress, off the charts. So it's no wonder that I got desperately, deathly ill with a 104-degree temperature and lost nine pounds in a week. That might have been a great diet program, but not really great on life! If I had not had the skills that I have—to be able to deconstruct the emotions, be able to put together a great supportive Five Star Formula and do a Target Plan for each area in which I was able to actually hit the target and work and make forward progress—I'm telling you I would've been suicidal.

But there is always a way out. I had no control over what my sisters thought, I had no control over my parents dying, I had no control over how they left the estate and what had to happen. I had no control over my husband leaving. So it's about how I chose, about how we all choose to *respond* to stress. You, as a coach, can make such an impact by helping your client choose how they will respond. It's really powerful. When things like this happen, and when things happen back to back like this, it's good to realize, "My life is not perfect. It doesn't always go exactly how I want it to go," and you have to pick yourself up by the bootstraps and make something happen.

THE HOLMES AND RAHE STRESS SCALE

I work with a whole lot of high-powered executives, in fact through the years that is probably the type of client I have worked with more than any other. The one thing they talk a lot about is *stress*. And the truth is we all have stress—good stress and bad. The alternative is you're six feet under. There is stress like, "Oh my God, I'm getting married! And the date is just one month away!" and "Oh my gosh, there's a jillion things to do..." It's all good, it's all fabulous, but *it is stressful!* "My daughter—she's having a baby! It's so exciting, it's so wonderful! Oh my gosh, we're moving! We're moving to the house of our dreams and oh my gosh, the windows aren't in yet! And I've got to furnish the thing! I've got to landscape the thing!" So the stress can be spectacular—it can be absolutely fabulous—but there are *not so great* areas of stress as well, right?

Psychiatrists Richard Rahe and Thomas Holmes studied over 5,000 patients and in 1967 announced a positive correlation between stress and illness[9]. Their "stress inventory" was called the "Holmes and Rahe Stress Scale (http://www.stress.org/holmes-rahe-stress-inventory/)." Researchers have subsequently done lots of research about

---

[9] https://en.wikipedia.org/wiki/Holmes_and_Rahe_stress_scale

stressful events in life and I love to give my clients this stress assessment because I then know what kind of stress they are under. Is it a great stress? Is it, "Oh my gosh, we're moving to our dream home and I'm getting married and I'm having a baby," and so on or is it "My husband just left me, my mom and my dad just died, I'm now battling with my sisters and no one is helping me. I have to clear out all the properties and they had four of them. I have to deal with all of the estate stuff." What kind of stress is that? What kind are we dealing with?

And stress does affect each of our bodies differently. This will be good for you as a coach to know and it will also help you help your clients so that you can help them in the area of health and vitality, you can help them in the area of focus, and you can help them start to have strategies so that they can get the plates all spinning in the air as opposed to all of them collapsing and falling and breaking around them. And for this reason, the Holmes Rahe stress assessment is one that I really love to use.

LOVE LANGUAGES ASSESSMENTS

Gary Chapman's *The Five Love Languages* is an incredible book. You'll find you will use what's in that book with your kids as well as with your spouse, as the book was definitely written with those relationships in mind. He has follow-up books such as *The Five Love Languages of Children, The Five Love Languages of Teenagers,* and many others, but I have found it really applies at work as well. So much in business and personal life is about relationships, whether it's your relationship with your body, your relationship with your colleagues, your relationship with your team, your relationship with your employees, your relationship with your wife or husband, your relationship with your children, your relationship with a grandchild. Life is about relationships, I don't care who or where you are. Sales is about relationships. And coaching is certainly about relationships.

The five love languages are:

1. Acts of service,
2. Words of affirmation,
3. Physical touch,
4. Quality time, and
5. Gifts

Chapman has free assessments online that you can take to figure out what the particular love languages are for the people in your own life. And this can be a real winner in business if you know that your boss's love language is "gifts," for example, and let me give you a hint—gifts can be as simple as a card. People who have "gifts" as their love language are not looking at price tags! They will keep every card, every Post-It note, every trinket that you ever drop on their desk. They will cherish it and keep it forever. In fact, "gifts" happens to be one of mine and I work in an organization where at the end of an event you always get this thank-you card, and I am devastated if I somehow get missed or overlooked to get my thank-you card. I have saved every single thank-you card I've ever gotten from every event from the last 20 years because that's a gift! So it's interesting how this actually works, and it's imperative to know this. It's not just some funny little thing to kind of play with.

People are usually drawn to having people in their lives who have different love languages. I'll give you an example: Take my brother-in-law and my sister. As life would have it, as fate would go, my sister's love languages are "quality time" and "acts of service." And here's what happens. My brother-in-law travels 90 percent of the time for his very high-powered, high earning, prestigious position. Guess what the result is? No time and no time to do acts of service. But *his* love language is "gifts," so he will come home with a mink coat from Saks Fifth Avenue in New York, with Godiva chocolates, with Tiffany and Cartier rings and jewelry—he will come home with all these amazing gifts. Guess where, on the ranking of the five love languages, gifts are for my sister? At the bottom, of course. She sees that as a waste of money and a waste of effort.

The idea is that your love language is the way in which you speak love or care to the people in your life. In the example with my sister, it's like one person is speaking Japanese and the other is speaking Greek and neither one of them can hear the other. When my sister wants to sit there on a three-week transatlantic cruise with my brother-in-law, my brother-in-law has two Blackberries out and he's tip-tapping his toes because time is his lowest love language. Now I will add that they have been married for 35 years for a reason. He has figured out that doing a three-week, quality time, transatlantic cruise speaks love to his wife. She has figured out that sports memorabilia means something to him, that a gift based around the San Francisco Giants is meaningful and fabulous, and that such a gift speaks love to him.

So for us coaches we need to figure out if we are speaking in our language or if we are speaking in a language that our client or our employee or our spouse or kids or friends will hear. Super important. Super valuable. And just doing a simple assessment will go very far.

PERSONALITY ASSESSMENTS

Regardless of which you use, I always do a personality assessment with clients. I have a belief that people are born with a bent towards one, or a combination or, usually, a predominance of a personality style. Your personality type does not incorporate habits and beliefs, and it doesn't incorporate values, but rather it's simply a way of being and a way that you sort through the world. Now, I didn't make this up. It became popular in the middle of the twentieth century that everyone in a corporation was doing every kind of personality assessment. As I said, I have studied most of them.

For example, there's the "DISC" assessment, there's the Myers-Briggs assessment, there's the temperament assessment, and there is the color code assessment (there is even an animal version of this). There are great books on the subject, and with just a little research, your knowledge of personality types will reap big rewards for both you and your clients.

PERSONALITY TYPES

This concept, that we each have a classifiable type, goes back to Hippocrates around 400BC. Hippocrates, that most famous doctor among the ancient Greeks, decided there were four distinct personalities—he called them *temperaments*—that came from the body fluids, the red blood, the bile, and so on.

- The yellow bile was the choleric.
- The red blood was the sanguine.
- The phlegm was the phlegmatic.
- Black bile was melancholy.

All personalities tend to fall predominantly into one of these four temperaments. Even so, most personalities tend to be blended, which I think is an important piece to remember. The four personality types (and how they fall into the DISC assessment) are:

1. Choleric "D"
2. Sanguine "I"
3. Phlegmatic "S"
4. Melancholy "C"

In the DISC assessment:

- the choleric, D is the dominant,
- sanguine, I, the influencer,

- phlegmatic, S is for steady,
- and the melancholy, C, is compliant.

I'm going to talk about these four personality types in a general manner because I'm not writing a book on personalities. There is so much good material out there, I don't know that I have to dive deep here. I'll go a mile wide and an inch deep so you have a sense of the personalities and if you're interested in this and want more you can go out and do some more reading. There are some hilarious books out there on this as well as some very scientific books on this, all written by different personalities of course! So the really studious ones are written by melancholies, and the hilarious, fun-laughing-at-human-nature ones written by the sanguine and influencers. I happen to know that because I know the authors. It's comical.

CHOLERIC

Let's talk about the choleric. Each one of these personalities has what I would call a tag line. The cholerics, the dominant Ds, the High Ds, these are the bosses of the world. Now it doesn't mean we don't have bosses in every personality type. We've had presidents, prime ministers, and all kinds of leaders of every personality. We have had, I'm sure, kings and queens and royalty in every personality. It doesn't mean you can't be these different roles in any personality but the *natural* person who is the boss, is the choleric. His or her tagline is, "*Do it my way now.* I'm right. I know, so just sit down and shut up, and go along with it." The funny thing is they do always think that they're right, and the sad part for the rest of us is nine times out of ten they are! They seem to know something about everything. Part of it is just in their nature to grab information about a lot of different things. They pay attention like that. They are definitely extroverts so they are what I would call "on the top side of the line"—outgoing while being very focused on the bottom line. When you're conversing with cholerics you want to make sure you condense, you don't tell stories. They just want the facts. You bullet point for them. If they want to know more they are going to ask, but don't offer it otherwise. They will go right to the bottom line.

The challenge with this person is he is like a bull in a china shop. He will run through, run over, wreak havoc, and leave a wake of carnage behind him or her. They don't listen. They hear three words and assume they know the rest of the sentence. They jump to conclusions and all of these things make them very difficult to work for or with. Yes, they are born leaders but if they don't mitigate some of their personality they make everybody insane along the way. They're tough to have on a team. They'll usually do what's called "seagull management"—fly over, crap all over, deliver their message and depart. Like helicopter parents, there's seagull management. There is opportunity, possibility to coach and help them, because any of these personality traits *can* be adapted and mitigated if you work and focus on them. Everyone has a style that they wear. In the old days the cholerics wore the power suits—perfect in style, with the red diagonal-striped tie. The women cholerics, they're wearing St. John's knit suits in black, navy, or Reagan red. Seriously, there's a look to these personalities. Most of the time I can see them coming and I know who they are. They dress the part.

SANGUINE

The sanguine is the person whose tagline is, "If we're doing this it's going to be fun, it's going to be a party!" The sanguine are party people. They're influencers. They'll sell spots to leopards and ice to Eskimos, and whatever other cliché you want to throw in there. Their whole objective is to make it all a game, make it fun. On a team they want everything to be like a game. The choleric likes competition—out to win and out to kill—but the sanguine wants it to be friendly competition, to get everybody involved, to get everyone engaged. They're the ones that put the Friday party together. They're gonna plan the celebration at the end of the week. And oh, my gosh, they are going to tell stories. In fact they're the ones who will come up to you and actually physically hold on to you to tell stories, they will not let you go. "Wait, wait, one more thing . . ."

While they will drive everyone nuts with this, the truth is they *are* fun. They will see the lighter side. They are quintessential optimists. They will naturally see what is great about everything. They will see the upside in things. They will be able to turn things around and make them fun. The challenge is you have to steer this person and you have to set the borders for them to play inside of, otherwise they will be all over the map. You've got to have a short leash of accountability with these people. If they are leading things they have to really learn to be specific and focused with the rest of their team or the rest of the team will have no comprehension, and the choleric on the team will think the sanguine is ridiculous. We've had presidents and prime ministers that were sanguine and they were very charismatic. In fact they are naturally charismatic. It's not something they strive for, it's just who they are by their nature. They wear color—they are the person who has got the Diane Freis dresses: multicolored, flaring skirts, ruffle sleeves. The

127

women who buy them are totally sanguine. Their clothing is fun and playful. That's just who they are by nature.

The negative is you need to keep them on track, you've got to get them to stop telling their stories. You've got to get them to the bottom line, which can be painful. It's something they've got to mitigate in order to really achieve things, to get to the end of things. By nature they are brilliant idea people, brilliant creatives, artistic, fun, and they need a team of people to finish anything because they are horrible finishers. Believe me, I have friends who are sanguine and they make me insane. They are absolutely on the top of the line, absolute extroverts.

PHLEGMATIC

The phlegmatics, the *steady* people, are whom I call the *vanilla*. They blend in with everybody. They are by nature below the line, they are introverts by nature. They're easy going. Their tagline is that they want peace, no matter what. They want harmony, so they will do whatever it takes to fill in all the gaps, to make everything work. They are people pleasers to the nth degree, whatever it takes to make everybody happy. Their goal in life is to ensure that everyone is happy, happy, happy, getting along and no waves. There are no tsunamis in this person's life. They make fantastic assistants and diplomats. They don't have an opinion on anything because they don't want to be on any side of the fence, so that everybody gets along.

And I'm sorry, they are the fillers of the world. They are the ones who get the project finished. They're the ones who do all the work and are happy doing that. All you do is give them praise and they're happy, happy, getting things done, not making any waves, and keeping things very peaceful in their life. Now here's the challenge with this: Because they never have an opinion they will never make a decision so don't ask them where we're going for dinner. Don't ask them what movie we're going to go see. Don't ask them where we're going on vacation, because that's an opinion and that means they're going to sit on one side of the fence or another, and that means, "Oh my gosh, somebody might not be happy with me and I might make a wave because it might not be what everybody wants to do."

And here's the other challenge with phlegmatics. Because they never want to make waves, they want peace and harmony so essentially, they will actually tell you what you want to hear, whether it's the truth or a lie. If they are backed into a corner they will actually lie and figure it will work its way out because they truly cannot stand not pleasing you and not telling you what you want to hear. This can be a challenge, obviously. Sometimes you need to hear the truth if there's a fire and the house is burning down and the project has gone to hell in a hand basket and you need to fix the project but they don't want to give the bad news.

MELANCHOLY

Our other introverts are the melancholies, and they are compliant people—"compliant" meaning following the rules, following the guidelines. They are policy and procedure executers. Their tag line is "If we're doing this it has to be done perfectly correctly—it's going to be done right." Now, that's great because we *need* people in this world who follow the rules and comply and have these guidelines to keep the sanguines in line and keeps the cholerics reporting so it's all straight up. These are our engineers, our analysts. They do all the research and compile all the facts and figures. They're CPAs and accountants. Thank goodness we have people who follow the rules, who put our taxes together and protect our money. Mine, recently, got me every single penny back because she followed every single guideline, every rule, so I could take every single deduction exactly perfectly right, and I know if I get audited there's not a problem. Everything is in its place, everything is accounted for, all the tables juggled and balanced and that's who you want in that position because they have natural skills to do that. Don't put *sanguines* in charge of your facts and figures because they're more like, "That's good enough," when it might be or might not be.

So our melancholy, as the word itself denotes, can seem a bit down because they are looking at what could be wrong. They have a propensity to be more gloomy, a little bit like Eeyore. They are kind of like the little black rain cloud because in the meeting they will tell you what is wrong with the plan. While you might paint the pie in the sky, announce all the great things that are going to happen, preach all the phenomenal and the beautiful things, this person, the melancholy, well it's his *job* to shoot holes in the whole thing so you know what could go wrong. So sometimes they come off as being kind of negative but the truth is they are just trying to protect you and everyone they care about. They are the risk economists in the world. They are going to protect us from where we might fall off the edge and keep us out of trouble but sometimes it comes off as negative.

So you want to be able to mitigate those tendencies and develop the capability of looking at what could be *great*.

PERSONALITY BLENDS

I want to talk a little bit about the *natural* blends and the *complementary* blends. The natural blends are the two extroverts, the choleric and the sanguine. Below the line there are the other natural blends, the two introverts, the phlegmatic and the melancholy. Those are the natural blends, and most everyone is some kind of a blend, to be honest. I find that in the natural blends you might have a high D who gets things done but knows how to mitigate all the stories and the goings on and is a high D blended. This is somebody who knows how to get things done and have fun doing it, so they are very charismatic leaders. Without getting into politics I will tell you that Bill Clinton is a sanguine-choleric, and Ronald Reagan was also a sanguine choleric. Barack Obama, for example, is a melancholy-choleric, a different blend.

Most people are a blend. Again, we've got natural blends and complimentary blends. The phlegmatic, remember, is the go-along person, and that phlegmatic really helps to mitigate the analytical and negative melancholy because they're more "go-along," and they are not sticklers. Now seriously, a strict, straight melancholy, if you don't follow the rules—I am not kidding you—they turn you in, they don't try to work it out, you broke the rules so you're going to jail and that's it. Now if somebody kills somebody that's one thing, but sometimes it's better for a team to work through things before you have a hammer come down on someone. So the phlegmatic is going to try to work things out and work things through and help through other means rather than just have the biggest hammer hit somebody on the head.

CHOLERIC-MELANCHOLY

The blends are very constructive. The complementary blends, like the choleric with the melancholy—man! These are workhorses. This is Barack Obama to be honest. They are head down, tail up, get the job done, really focused on projects, focused on being productive, focused on production, focused on those outcomes. I think Donald Trump is such a blend. Steve Wynn of the Wynn Hotels is absolutely this personality type. He is a perfectionist but man, he is a get-it-done person. He doesn't get stuck in the periphery of all that. He is someone who's really learned to mitigate all of that and to celebrate his staff's wins, his staff's perfection, his staff doing things right. Oh, it's amazing!

SANGUINE-PHLEGMATIC

Another blend is the sanguine-phlegmatic. This is someone who is very easy going, very fun to have around, great to have on board as staff. They are an interesting blend to have as a parent. They're not big on results but they are big on love and forgiveness and creating a warm home space, and man, this is your quintessential, amazing Mother Earth, this I-F type. We had a restaurant chain out here in California for a long time

133

called Marie Calendar's. Now Don, her son, started the restaurant but Marie was the Mother Earth and mother of all the people that held it altogether, and she was totally an I-F. Don, of course, was that D-I. He was charismatic but the get-it-done guy.

ALL KINDS

So as far as these blends go, you want everybody on your team. It takes all the personalities to get all the great projects and jobs done, to get a company to really operate. And when you hire, and when you expand your team, you want to think about not having more of *you*—which is the mistake most people make—but really hiring on people who complement you. Ask yourself, "What am I missing? What do I need to have? What am I not great at that I need to have someone else do?" Do you need somebody more analytical than you? Do you need somebody who will get along and help cement the whole team together and keep that harmony? All of these are super-important pieces.

PERSONALITIES AT WORK

Every one of these personalities (and combinations) has their strengths, and every one of these personalities has their *limitations*—I don't call them *weaknesses,* because I do think we can mitigate those. And what you want to notice in your coaching is literally every strength, and notice them to an extreme, because these become a barricade. They become the block. They become the hurdle you need to get over and around or under or through *because it's too much of it.* Too much fun with this sanguine, and you get nothing done. Too much of just push, push, push, push, push, makes everyone on edge, makes everyone frustrated and angry and overwhelmed. Too much perfection of an analysis, too much of that little black rain cloud, and honestly no one wants to play with you. And too much of just going along and just making peace when it's not the truth is also not good. So we need to learn what our areas of strength are that can become barricades; what are the hurdles that we need to get under, around, or through? Where are they? I have all of my clients do a personality assessment so that at I know right off the bat who they are at their core. It's not like I go in immediately and work on that, but as they have challenges I know exactly what's going on with them!

ADAPTING

Those strengths that have gone overboard, that have gone to the extreme, you have to work through, you have to work out with your client. You've got to get over, around, and through. You need to mitigate them and learn to *adapt*. You also want our client to understand these personalities because you want them to understand that their teammates are not going to be like them, that they are going to have different challenges and different struggles, and that they are going to need to be working, helping their teammates to understand that, and to work through those things so that they can help them to adapt, too.

In talking about adapting, there are several ways in which the melancholy, for example, needs to be not so nit-picky, and not hitting people like a hammer over the head all the time for not following all the rules—not that they don't follow rules or guidelines, but just that they understand why people like the choleric are thinking, "This is going to be good enough—we're at 80 percent and the momentum will carry us the rest of the way." You can understand that this is part of the choleric's nature. And then, there are times the choleric needs to understand that you do need to go 100 percent, that sometimes a "good enough" isn't good enough, that the race isn't over until you've gone 26.2 miles.

COMMUNICATION STYLES

All of these personalities, you can see, have areas where they need to learn to flex and adapt. They all have, because of their strengths, different communication styles. I have alluded to some of these because it's so much a part of their nature, but it's important because in the work world (and I work with so many people on their businesses, with so many executives on how they should work with their staff in order to be effective) communication styles definitely matter. So with the choleric, for example, who just wants the bottom line, he needs to realize that if he's communicating with a melancholy, that melancholy is going to feel incomplete and unheard if they haven't been able to give details—that person is all about detail. And if the choleric is communicating with a melancholy, he or she needs to realize that melancholy *needs* the details. You can't just skip over it all and give a big, broad overview. That's not enough for them and they will not feel communicated with.

By the same token, if the choleric just comes in like a bull in a china shop the phlegmatic is going to shy away in the corner, and be pressed to tell them what they want to hear. It's going to cause that phlegmatic to have a knee-jerk reaction to actually lie to make that person happy. So the choleric here needs to give the phlegmatic space, give them time, allow them to ask questions. You—the choleric in this case—need to change your physiology and communicate so the phlegmatic feels like it is safe to tell the truth, to tell what is really going on. In the end the choleric will be glad, but initially it is not the nature of the choleric. They tend to push, push, push, quick, quick, quick, tell me, tell me, tell me, and that phlegmatic is going to be pushed right into a corner. And the phlegmatic or the choleric need to realize in communicating with a sanguine, that the sanguine is going to want to tell stories. The choleric is going to need to help them, to allow a *little* bit of that, and to steer them to the point in a gracious way. They're going to want to focus on what's fun about this or how can we make this a game; or to get projects done, how can we make this a friendly competition? You're going to get the most out of your sanguines if you do that.

Sanguines need to realize the rest of the world does not need to hear those stories. They need to get to the bottom line with the choleric. The choleric will ask for more details if they need them. The sanguine, when communicating with the phlegmatic (who is the easiest one for a sanguine to communicate with, because they won't push the phlegmatic into a corner), if they want cooperation, needs to make sure the friendly competition is not too intense, that it's very friendly, there is no losing, and you've got harmony going on.

With the melancholy, the sanguine needs to realize that all the flowery stories are not important. If the sanguine can learn how to tell their story with facts and details the melancholy's going to be thrilled.

The phlegmatic needs to realize he's the only guy trying for peace everywhere, that he needs to give details and facts that are true and even scientific to the melancholy. With the sanguine he needs to be a little bit playful, not so introverted, needs to raise energy a little bit, and needs to get to the bottom line and tell the truth to the choleric. The melancholy needs to learn that not everyone wants all the details—in fact, *none* of the other personalities want any of that. They need to stop being sticks in the mud and learn it's not all about following the rules, that honestly, we don't need any more rules, we've got enough rules.

Melancholies really need to understand that the rest of the people are not lying and cheating if they don't follow *all* the rules to the letter of the law. In California we have a thing called a "California Stop," and it makes melancholies insane. If you don't stop at a stoplight and pause for half a minute, you are breaking the law. Every other personality will roll right through that thing if they don't see a police officer-- which is the California Stop. The rest of the personality types do not see that as breaking the law.

RAPPORT

It's important to understand that there are different communication styles. You want to be in rapport with the people you're working with. In sales, you want to have rapport with the person and you want to make the sale. If you want to get the outcome of a sale, then you'd better adapt to the person's communication style that you are working with. When I worked in real estate, knowing these personalities helped in a huge way to win every sale. I would paint a picture of life and how fun it was going to be for the sanguine, I would get straight to the bottom line and be completely logic-based with choleric. I would give every fact and every detail, and dot every "i" and cross every "t" with the melancholy, and I would accentuate how family-oriented, how smooth, how easy, how peaceful the whole transaction was going to be and how we were going to create more peace, more cooperation, more harmony in their life to the phlegmatic. Everybody is selling something, and in sales you want to think about these personalities. You have to adapt to people and the way you communicate is the first way you adapt.

PERSONALITIES IN RELATIONSHIPS

Of course, personalities in relationships can be very funny. Each has strengths and limitations in a marriage or with their kids.

MORE ASSESSMENTS

I've covered why I do assessments as well as the cause and effect aspects of habits, and I've covered a good deal about personality types. All of this is really important. I've also discussed stress. Along the way I mentioned a book (a series, really) titled *The Five Love Languages*. I want to credit Gary Chapman, the author, who has done a brilliant job. In fact I think that's an important assessment for people, even in business. He's also got an assessment for kids, one for parents, for teens, for spouses and singles, as well as business people and colleagues. I had taken a course in *Love Languages* and previously had no idea they went into all these different aspects. It's so fascinating how bosses and their employees, normally know nothing about these available assessments or about what is taught in *Love Languages*; and how many know about *Love Languages* and never think about applying them at work. My gosh, what if your employees really need quality time with you? If you never meet with them, if you never see your employees, if you're just firing off a text message from time to time when what they really want is quality time, think about how you would get more buy-in if you actually gave your employees time!

Or gifts! And let me tell you, for people for whom gifts are their thing, it's very, very important that you give them little notes, little tokens, a Starbucks card, a little gift card, a card for their birthday, a Post-It with a "Well done!" or an "Atta' boy!" Those are all—seriously—gifts. If gifts are their thing, anything you give them is a gift, even if it's just a great note.

Something that is also super important that I've discovered and is relatively new is explained in a book titled *Positive Intelligence* by Shirzad Chamine. He's a professor from Stanford who has a number of Ted Talks out that are absolutely fantastic. He has an assessment on what he calls a "positive quotient" or "PQ." He has another whole assessment on saboteurs—on what's sabotaging you and great explanations, and these two assessments take a total of seven minutes to do them both. You will find out what it is that's stopping you and what is likely to trip you up. I think it's very important for a coach and a client or an employer and an employee to know what's going to stop your employee. What's going to stop your work force? What are the things that are just naturally going to trip them up? Are they, for example, achievers and they just go, go, go and they're scattered everywhere and they can't sit still for two seconds to actually listen, or are they procrastinators? What's going to stop their work? What's going to sabotage their success? It's a super-important assessment. I think it's really, really, valuable.

So assessments are valuable tools and there are so many good ones. Some more are:

- the temperaments assessment by *Personality Plus* author Florence Littauer which is brilliant
- a similar assessment on temperaments by Tim LaHaye, author of *Spirit-Controlled Temperament*
- the DISC, that has been hugely popularized, also on the temperaments
- the Color Code Personality Profile, also called simply The Color Code or The People Code, which was created by Dr. Taylor Hartman. This assessment divides people and personalities into four colors:
  - red for those motivated by power,
  - blue for those motivated by intimacy,
  - white if motivated by peace,
  - and yellow those motivated by fun;

- and of course there is the Myers-Briggs for personalities.

All of them work. All of them are assessments and assessing is very, very, important for several reasons. You want to know how people are naturally going to operate, and you want to know how they are going to compromise themselves. You want to know how people are going to adapt—What are they going to do to adapt? What's going to slide what direction? Is the dominant person (in the DISC, for example) going to get angrier and more forceful and more bossy or is he going to adapt it down and play more? As an employer you want to know what people are going to do. If you are a partner, you want to know what your partner is going to do.

Here's the thing we need to understand. The first client that you ever have, the first person that you ever want to take a look at to find out what their saboteurs are, what their positive quotient is, how stressed out they are and what they're going to do to adapt, what their personality strengths are, where their compromises are, where their challenges are going to be, where they're going to be tripped up—in communication or in the work force, for example—the first person that you need to be looking at and be concerned with is obviously yourself. Don't be ordering other people around to do some of these assessments if you have not experienced them first, because the truth is *you* are your first client. You want to know what your strengths are yourself, and what your limitations are as well. What is going to trip you up? What is going to sabotage you?

I just want to underscore these other assessments. In fact scholars are coming up with new assessments all the time, and the *Positive Intelligence* one is so very important. And what's awesome is that you are not stuck! None of this is what you are necessarily born with. It's just what you've got to work with and improve upon.

KEY 4: TRANSFORM

A Neat Ornamented, or Town Coach

THE FOURTH KEY OF coaching is the transformation step. Once you have an idea of who your client is, you now want to start to get cognizant to where you want to make shifts and changes. You will want to reflect on whether or not their values serve them, and if their beliefs serve them. This is where you start to compare who they are with what the person wants. Once you start exploring and they start talking about what's important to them, and what they think about and what's true for them (which is their values and beliefs), and once they actually start to explore their identity and start speaking to "I am this," and "I am that," and once they start doing these assessments and their personality profile and they look at their positivity quotient -- it's funny, the changes already start to happen. This is because the first step of change is awareness.

Now your client becomes totally open and aware and conscious. They've been running around until now unconscious, just stressed out and not really understanding why things haven't been working and why they have not been achieving what they have said they want to achieve; and why they have not been going in the direction they really want to go; or why they've been going in five directions and not achieving any one certain thing. It's because they were running around with conflicts. They've had conflicting values or conflicting beliefs and they were focusing on what they don't want instead of what they do want. It's pretty hilarious how this can all work.

So this is where you start really looking, asking, "What are the values and are there conflicts?" Is one saying "I want to go north," while at the same time saying, "I want to go south"? Your client can't do both, not at one time. What are they believing? Do they believe, "I love all people except I don't want to do anything with those type of people or that race, or that creed, or that color, or whatever." It's not that

I'm promoting that way of thinking, I'm just pointing out that what shows up in these clients is they've got these rules that are stopping them from going in the direction they say they want to go in.

VALUES & BELIEFS

You start, then, to look at this and help your client ask themselves, "For where I want to go, for what I want my life to be about, for the goal that I've set for the week, the year, or for the next 10 years, what needs to be important to me? What values do I need to have? And to back that up what do I need to believe in order to achieve that?" If they want to take care of all women who are baby boomers and make sure that they have a second chance at life after they've had their kids and the career they wanted; or maybe they took the career that was sort of handed to them and they want to change and do what they are passionate about; and yet they say, "Yeah, but I don't like those kind of people. I don't like that race or..." Well, that's pretty conflicting. That's not going after everyone, that's not helping everyone, that's helping everyone *except*. They have to consciously ask themselves, "Is that what my rule is, really? Is that really what I want to be about? Is that really how I'm going to market myself? Is that really how I want my avatar to be?"

You're now going to ask conscious questions and your client is going to write down what is important to them. They are going to write down answers to, "What do I need to believe?" After you've captured values and beliefs, and they start to look at their needs and ask themselves, as a mature adult, as a human being who wants to be completely actualized, "What need needs to show up? What's the human need that I need to put first? What needs drive me?" Maybe before it was all about, "I'm going to play the martyr and just give everything away," and as a result they have nothing and can't take care of their own family. It's like, unless they are a saint and just giving everything away trusting that everything is going to be taken care of, and they really do want to make a difference, then they may want to have some goals and be smart about their contribution.

Maybe significance has been driving them and being important as been driving them, but it's been in an immature way where it's "Pick me! Pick me!" They're waving their hand, "Pay attention to me! I'm going to drive a red, flashy Ferrari. I'm going to spend all my money looking good so you can think I'm something!" as opposed to, "I'm going to really make a contribution to people. I'm going to make a difference and I'm going to let the reports of those people whose lives are changed be my calling card." Really asking themselves what's going to be the thing that they are known for, that they are important for, and *have significance in that way* drive them. So they want to decide: values, beliefs, and their driving need that they *choose* in order to get the result they really desire to have.

PERSONALITY

Then you look at the next portion of this, which is their personality. You need to really dive in and look at, "Hey, there is a strength!" We have had presidents and prime ministers of every predominate personality type. With every one of these personality types, whether a choleric or high-D or sanguine or an I, or a phlegmatic S or a melancholy C, all of them can be a president or prime minister or a general manager or an entrepreneur or an owner of a major corporation. They all have strengths and they all have limitations or challenges. So you want to look at what people's strengths are and really call them to action. What are the things that you really want to have show up? You're going to point those out and you're going to start designing some conscious thought as to what they want to accentuate. Then of course you want to look at, "What do you want to limit? What do you want to diminish? What do you want to have play smaller?"

THE CHOLERIC

I'll give an example. One of the strengths of a high-D personality, a choleric personality, is that they are born leaders. If you're in a group of 20 people left in a room and someone has said, "Well, you guys need to make a presentation and we want to see it in an hour," and you're all just looking at each other, that high-D personality is going to take charge immediately and start to lead and direct. So that's a great strength, and here's what happens. As a limitation they start getting angry if you don't follow them and they start bossing everybody around. They're very directive and they're not very engaging. So it's really important that they learn how their strengths could be great and how to diminish some of those traits that are not so great.

PHLEGMATIC

I'll take the polar opposite of that for another example. The phlegmatic S (steady) is really wonderful as a team member. My gosh they will get along, they will totally help collaborate, they don't push and shove, they will engage other people, they're all for going along with other ideas, and they make fabulous rank-and-file. But here's the challenge! Somebody needs to make a decision! Somebody needs to take charge!

They need to learn that sometimes the job is to step up and be in charge. Sometimes it means, man, oh man, they've got to decide! They've got to decide, do you want A or B or C? Choose! Because they're not good at making decisions, not good at pulling the trigger, not good at stepping up. That's not their trait. It's a limitation they need to own. They have to make a conscious choice and step in and lead at times.

CREATING IDENTITY

So that's just two extreme examples to play with. I could go through all the personalities and give great examples of what they're wonderful at, but the beginning of transformation is to really evaluate this, to really look at this and to really start to compare and contrast who they are with who they want to be. So the next piece, naturally, would be to create the identity that is going to help them achieve what they want. Who do they need to be? That's a great question. "Who do I need to be in order to get XYZ results? Who do I need to be to lead the team? What characteristics must I demonstrate on a daily basis?" This is the part of the process where you really start to call up these forward-thinking questions and really have your client pay attention to themselves and listen to what the pieces are that they need to embrace and embody. "What's the identity that I need that will give me that one-year goal in a relationship, or in my business, or in my health and vitality? What identity do I need to embrace and really embody in order for me to hit that target at the end of five years or at the end of 20 years?" Most everyone arrives *somewhere* in 20 years. And here's the question your client needs to ask themselves: "Am I the person I need to be to help me land where it is I actually hope and wish and dream that I will land in 20 years?" They're going to be somewhere—most likely they are going to be somewhere—and the question is: Are they the person that can take them where they want to go? And here's the thing I said before, and it bears repeating: We are not born with an identity, we *create* an identity, and usually it is by default.

This is the point where you evaluate, you look at what your client's needs and values and beliefs are, and at what their personality and identity in the past has been. Are all those congruent with where they want to go next? It is super important to ask that question to get them to design -- actually purposefully design -- who it is that they need to be. A simple question can be, "Who do you need to be in order to get to that result? It can be a list of traits and characteristics that they need to embody in order to be there. Transformation starts to come through and it will when you get into the execution and implementation, but right now you need to design it, and you need to come up with it.

THE RIGHT QUESTIONS

And there's one more piece in this transformation. We all have self-talk. I will mention this again when we get into the Five-Star Formula—that formula for every emotional state—inside of which we have self-talk. We all have the chatterbox up in our brain and most of the time (I am told that men don't have it going all of the time and that women do) it's chattering away, saying something. And here's the sad thing: very often—I can't say that I have a statistic for exactly what the percentage is—the questions we are asking in our brain are not powerful, they are not helpful, they are not questions to really get us to where we really truly want and need to go.

DISEMPOWERING QUESTIONS

A *dis*empowering question might be:

- What's wrong with me?
- Why does this always happen to me?
- Why does it always go wrong?
- Why don't they like me?

Disempowering chatter is obviously not helpful. They are not questions to really get your client to where they truly want and need to go.

EMPOWERING QUESTIONS

Samples of great questions are:

- Hmm, what has to happen for me to get that result?
- What's the most powerful thing that I could be doing today?
- What's the thing that I can do today to get that result that I'm aimed at?
- What's the one thing that would help catapult me forward towards that goal that I've got for the week?
- What's great about this?
- If I were to enjoy what I do, what would be enjoyable?
- What would I love about this?
- What do I love about that person?
- What is great about that person?
- What's an upside of this situation?
- What's a win that I can take away from this?

Those are all filtering questions that are very positive, very powerful, and will change the stress level in a person's body. This will change your client's life, and it will change their health. It will change their vitality, asking powerful questions as opposed disempowering questions.

Once you go on through that whole evaluation stage and determine what new values they want to hold true, and have them ask, "What's the least that I need to have? What's the need that I really want to drive me? What are my personality strengths and where do I need to diminish those limitations?", they can get conscious and then design an identity that's going to embrace all of that – and you can start asking powerful questions. The transformation will have begun through all of those pieces. Change is now happening, change is taking place.

CHOOSING EMOTIONS

Questions asked, awareness and change begun, you are now at the bridge that takes you into what I call the Five Star Formula. I'm going to get into the details of shifting your client's emotional state so that it *supports* them, because underneath everything, they can have all the best intentions, having a very constructed driving need, building on strengths, diminishing limitations, having strong, fabulous, congruent values; but if their emotional state is a complete wreck with depression and sadness driving them, none of it going's to work. So, you want to manage their *emotional state* and you want them to be in a place where their emotional state is giving them what they want. The foundation under everything is the emotional state for sure.

Again, a person can have all the best goals, plans, strategies in the world, but if they do not have an emotional state that will support them, nothing else matters, to be honest. So it's really important to know that nobody *makes* someone else feel angry, nobody else on the planet. I hear this all the time, "Oh, she makes me so angry. Oh, she just totally makes me just hate! She just makes me so depressed," or, "This makes me so depressed." Well, no. Emotions are a choice. We *choose* our emotional state. We choose depression. We choose sadness. And we can choose excitement. We can choose enthusiasm. We can choose love. We can choose kindness.

So, once your client has chosen the emotion they want, you can then do the Five Star Formula and help them *create it, they can create the life they want.*

My Two Wheelhouses: The Target Plan and the Five Star Formula

Here is the Five Star Formula for deconstructing or constructing an emotion:

1. Physiology (5 components)
2. Self Talk
3. Beliefs
4. Focus
5. Meaning

When I've discovered patterns, and when I've seen that people are having what I would call identity, belief, or emotional challenges; or rather, when they're being stopped—and that's the root of it—when they've got conflict in their identity, it means they've got conflict in their beliefs or they have conflicting values. I call that an *emotional barrier* that they've got. And when their emotional state is what's stopping them I then go to the Five Star Formula. Recognizing an emotional barrier triggers for me, as a coach, that the tool I'm going to pull out of my tool belt is the Five Star Formula. This doesn't mean that I don't have other tools to utilize, but this is my go-to tool.

In addition to the Five Star Formula, another go-to tool is the Target Plan. When I have somebody who has a target, a goal, and an objective that they're struggling with, and they can't get motivated or figure out where they're going, and they're feeling overwhelmed -- *busy* but not getting stuff done—I immediately go to a *Target Plan*. This is because, as you'll see, all the ways to be motivated, all the ways to actually motivate someone into action and get real motives, are in this formula. (We'll talk about the Target Plan when we get into execution and implementation). But if you're not overly concerned with emotions as a barrier, if you simply need to get things clear, to deconstruct an outcome that your client has, I pull out the Target Plan because you can get clarity and see exactly how to get to where they want to go. They can get out of just being busy and action-oriented.

So those are my two wheelhouses, the Five Star Formula and the Target Plan. Inside all of that I am always considering people's personalities, where they are in the Psychle of Performance (covered in Key 2, Explore), and all of the other things I cover in this book. All of these tools and aspects of a client are in consideration during my coaching, even while I, the coach, am following the steps of a coaching call. It's an *art*, coaching, but there are *science* pieces to it that help it, so you can replicate success. Make sense?

THE FIVE STAR FORMULA

PHYSIOLOGY
- WALK
- TALK
- STANCE
- BREATH
- FACE EXPRESSION

SELF-TALK
- WHAT ARE YOU SAYING TO YOURSELF?

BELIEFS
- WHAT DO I BELIEVE ABOUT THAT?

FOCUS
- WHAT ARE YOU THINKING ABOUT?
- WHAT ARE YOU FOCUSED ON?

MEANING YOU MAKE UP
- WHAT ARE YOU MAKING THINGS MEAN?
- "SO WHAT"

THE FIVE STAR FORMULA is a way to *deconstruct* an emotional state someone finds him or herself in—any emotional state—and also it is a way to *construct* an emotional state. The way this makes sense in coaching is that we often find people in an emotional state that is not serving them. They're depressed or they're sad, they're just stuck in grief, or they are angry, or they're bitter or they're frustrated, or, what is really most normal is they're a combination, they're not just one thing. You've got three or four or even five of those all thrown in together.

It turns out there are five elements of an emotion and you can start at any element and one will lead to the next. By deconstructing a person's emotional state you can actually see how these *five* different elements of emotion fit together. One thing leads to the next, leads to the next, leads to the next. So if, all of a sudden, your client finds him or herself in an emotional state they don't want to be in, there is something you can do about it.

Emotional states are usually unconscious, which is just the human condition of how we operate. And what's great news is that all of that is a *habit*. The truth is a habit is something that is learned, it's not something you have to be in. Your emotions are something you choose (even if it's an unconscious choice), so you can determine your own, determine to take on emotions that serve rather than disempower you. One of the things I love about coaching is that we can actually help people *construct* an emotional state. Usually it is a stack of two or three, maybe four emotions that they choose, emotions that will serve them and help them get to where they want to go, to create what they want to create.

I will also say that if someone's emotional state is really stopping them -- like being depressed or angry or just stressed out, overwhelmed, bitter, or frustrated -- if they're in an emotional state like that they're not likely, in that state, to be able with just a Target Plan to make anything happen that they want to make happen. So it's really important to be aware, if somebody, for example, has a goal of building a business of an online funnel and getting people to opt in and buy their products, and they're not in an emotional state that's going to support that, then you're wasting their time, your time, and all of the energy going into that business plan. I mean you're much better off, really, just working on this piece first if you want to get a result. Now some clients come in and they're already so jazzed, so stoked, so excited and they're in a great emotional state to get the results they want. If that's the case, no problem! You can absolutely go right into a Target Plan. It just depends. There are reasons then as to why and what you do first with someone.

In no specific order, because you can actually create or deconstruct an emotion starting with any point of the Five Star Formula, where all the points are equal, let's see what the five points or elements are. Again, you can start in with any point you like or prefer in applying this. The five elements that determine a person's emotion, the five equal points of the Five Star Formula are:

1. Physiology
2. Focus
3. Beliefs
4. Self-Talk
5. Meaning

PHYSIOLOGY

We'll talk about physiology first because I find that my own emotional state really, truly starts with physiology. I have clients who that's not true for, but let's start with it nonetheless. There happen to also be *five* components to your physiology:

- how you walk,
- how you talk,
- your breathing,
- facial expressions,
- and your stance.

There are aspects to each of these—walking, for example. Are you walking *direct?* Are you walking *fast?* Pounding your feet? Or, are you wandering, sauntering? All the different ways one might walk, with the pace, force, speed, all of that determines and will be different with different emotional states. How you talk has a pace, volume, also has articulation, timbre, tone. In fact there are about five or six aspects of how we talk. Each of those—like if you talk very softly, hesitantly, running your words together—have an emotional state attached to them. But if you talk with articulation, if you talk with volume and pace, there's a speed and a force to it, and that's a very different emotion you portray. It's interesting that there are different emotions that parallel different ways of breathing, even.

Now here's what's incredible with physiology. It is universal. I have been in events where I have watched a demonstration of this, done by two people. One person puts himself into an emotional state, consciously thinking about it, and the other person mirrors that and matches it and tries to copy it exactly. The person who copies it will be able to tell the person in that emotional state exactly what's going on, to the point of where they are and everything, how they're feeling, all to the tee. Emotions have very specific physiology, and all they're matching in that exercise, is the physiology. They don't have any information other than that. They're

165

matching the facial expression, they're matching the stance, they're matching the vocal quality, every single piece of that, and when they do they'll have the exact emotional state.

To further break it down, every emotion has its own specific physiology. I watched an entire theater full of people acting out depression, and they slumped forward. Their muscles went lax, their shoulders fell forward, their heads went down, everyone. They all did the same exact thing. It's like the whole collective height of the audience went down a foot. Now, you do excitement, with the same audience and guess what? Everyone gets taught and tense, and every head is up. The shoulders are back and the whole audience just got a foot taller. So it's important to realize that if you want to relate to anyone, or if you want your client to have a certain emotion, they definitely have to have a certain physiology.

FOCUS

The second point (and the order is of no importance), is *focus*. Where is your attention? What are you thinking about? What are your thoughts on? Are your thoughts on great things? Are your thoughts on things that are going to go wrong? What are you thinking about? I can guarantee that what you're thinking about is going to affect every other piece of this emotional state. If you're focused on things being negative, on things going wrong, anything like that, I guarantee you everything is going to be reflected like that. And you're going to get that emotional state.

For example, if you're focused on getting a bad test score, if you're focused on not getting the promotion or not winning the project, if you're focused on how bad you did in the presentation, I guarantee you that's going to affect your emotional state which will affect the result. Now if you're focused on how great it is and all the stuff that went right, and what was wonderful about it, and what went right about it and all the pieces you felt competent about or what pieces you're assured of and so on, that is also going to affect the result. So what are you focused on?

BELIEFS

Now, the next piece—and it's kind of like they start running one into the other—is, "What are your beliefs?" You're making statements in your head, so are they what you believe? What do you believe to be true? What was great about it, or what sucked about it? What could go wrong? Are you believing that, "Oh, my gosh there's so much traffic I'm never going to make it and they're going to hate me and..."

Where are those thoughts—your focus—going, and what do you believe? What beliefs are you making up, and it's *all made up,* by the way. In fact, I have a friend who named his web site "itsallmadeup.com." It is all made up! Those beliefs will lead to an emotional state. So if you believe that you're not going to get the promotion, that they're not going to like what you said, they're not going to think you're of value, believe me, you're going to contribute to that and your emotional state will be down. That of course affects your physiology and all of that starts to affect each other.

SELF-TALK

Another piece of this after we've got physiology, focus, and beliefs—three of the five so far—is self-talk. Everyone on the planet, if they're honest, has a chatterbox going on upstairs. They're saying all kinds of things to themselves. In coaching what we'd like to do is train the client to actually control and steer the chatterbox, to put a governor on the chatterbox so the chatterbox is only saying things that will contribute to the action of obtaining what we desire; but we all know that sometimes that little self-talk goes on and on and on in a very haphazard, harmful direction where we don't actually want to go.

So it's kind of hairy and scary that we do that, but again, what are you saying to yourself? We've got our thoughts, which is where our focus is going, and that goes right along with what we are saying to ourselves and what our beliefs are. Do we believe that it's all going to work out? Do we believe it's all going to crumble? Do we believe that it's going to go to hell in a hand basket? Do we believe that we're going to be successful? Do we believe that we can do it? Do we believe that we are going to fail? It's what we're saying—all of those things—that gives weight to our focus and our beliefs.

MEANING

The fifth piece of this is a little harder to capture sometimes. As human beings we are meaning-making machines. We make meaning out of everything. "Oh, they didn't talk to me. I didn't get an invitation to that event. They didn't even mention my name . . ." And you're making it mean what? "Oh they don't like me. They don't want me to be a part of that." Now none of that is probably true, but we make all sorts of stuff up and we are making meaning out of all of it. All the focus, the beliefs, and the self-talk, will lead us from our *perspective* that we're experiencing. We're making it mean "xyz," whatever it is we've just made up. Sometimes pieces of it have some truth. Some of it can be completely irrelevant. Some of it may have no bearing in the realm of truth. So it's really important to realize that we can make things mean great stuff and we can make things mean the world is over as we know it. We can go any direction with this.

APPLICATION

Let me give a few examples of how I use the Five Star Formula. Let's say I've got somebody who really wants to make things happen, and I notice that their physiology, even from their voice on the phone, is really down, really not engaged, and everything really leads me to think I don't know how this person is going to make this happen. So I ask this person to describe how they are feeling. Not the story but how they would label the emotion they are in right now. Let's pretend they say they are agitated or in overwhelm or frustrated. Let's just say they came up with two or three things that are like that.

First of all I want to change their physiology. So assuming they are sitting, I have them stand up. I have them shake that all out. I have them actually stand like they are agitated. Then I add, "Stand like you are overwhelmed." There are slight differences, keep in mind. I have them describe their physiology by asking them, "How is your head? How are your shoulders? How is the tension in your gut? How is the tension in your legs? How are your legs—are you on one foot, on both feet? Is your weight distributed in that stance?" Then I have them describe, "What is your facial expression, and is there a shift in those emotions or is it fairly constant, kind of a cumulative effect of the emotion?" After they've done that I have them stay in that state and describe how they are breathing.

So we kind of get an assessment. I have them describe their physiology by asking them, "If you were to walk across the room in this state, how does your body move? Is it slow, is it direct, is it moderate? Is it wandering? Is it on purpose? What's the force in it? Is it heavy or light?" Because emotions are different. I assess whether they are able to describe all of that and I have them explain, "In this state, tell me, what are you thinking about? What are you focused on in this emotional state?" They'll often tell me they're focused on what's not working, that they're doing poorly, or they're anxious about a report that's gonna come out, focused on a bad review they're going to get, they're upset about what their children have done and what's not happening, and how they're out of control and so on. I ask them, "In this emotional state *what do you believe is true?*" Not "Is it true?" but "What do you believe? Stay in this emotional state with that focus, and what do you believe?" And they will tell me things like, "I believe I will not be successful at this. I believe I could get fired. I believe I'm not going to get a good report or get the raise. I believe that my kids are going to be in trouble and I can't help them." All these things come up.

So I then say, "Alright, so what are you *saying* to yourself? What's the chatter that's going on? What's the self-talk that's in your head?" And they'll give me things like, "I'm not worthy of the job. I'm not going to be successful. I'm a failure." They're normally very *identity* focused, and in this case, focused on what's not working. It leads to, "What are you making this mean?" And it leads to emotions that have to do with self worth and with the lack of success, the hopelessness, the worthlessness, or whatever it is.

So once I see this, I instruct them, "Now shake that off." I have them jump up and down and actually shake it off, and shift their weight to the other foot. See, *motion creates emotion.* Our emotions are inside of our musculature, and if you find yourself constantly in a weird emotion, I would sit a different way. Cross your legs a different way. Put your weight on a different foot. If you shift, your emotion will shift.

So now we decide, "What's the emotion that you would like to have? What's the emotion that you want to live in? We put that emotional state in the center of the star, and usually there are two or three: "I would like to be calm, I would like to be excited. I would like to feel enthusiastic," are just a few examples. Sometimes it's very interesting, the emotions they give you. They often don't sound like they go together but it's an interesting balancing act and combination of energy. And that's how we are in the world. We're not often in *an* emotion, we're often in a combination of them. We are in several at the same time: excitement, maybe anticipation, and centered or calm, for example. There's balancing.

So we then go through this process again and I tell them, "Now, you're calm, excited, and enthusiastic, and I want you to stand like that. Describe how you're standing. Describe your facial expression." It's a completely different muscle tension. It's a completely different facial expression, completely different way of breathing. And we go through the process: "Stay in that state. Now what are you thinking about? What are you focused on?"

"Well, I'm focused on what I could do next. I'm focused on the plan! I'm focused on great action. I'm focused on the results!" It's amazing how this starts to shift.

"And what do you believe when you're in that emotional state, that excitement, enthused, calm? What do you believe in that place?"

"Well I believe I can do it. I believe—you know I believe there will be some challenges, but I believe that there's hope, I believe I can fix things, I believe I can take action, I believe I can take part."

"So what are you saying to yourself?"

"I'm saying things like, I can stick with this! I can stay with the plan. If that doesn't work I'm going to try something different."

It's a very different way of looking at things and from the self-talk you start saying, "Okay what are you now making things mean?"

"You know what? That *I can do things.* That if the plan doesn't work I can create a new plan. You know, I'm really hopeful! That I'm going to be able to make progress. That I can be productive. That it may take some time but I can get to the result."

So now it's shifted dramatically and *in this emotional state we can then go into a Target Plan* and really make things happen. So it's really critical to have the recipe, to have the formula for the "five stars" so you can get an emotional state that will *help* the plan that your client wants to execute. This is the foundation that backs them up.

HUMAN EMOTION

Everyone, because we are human, has the full span of emotions, even big name celebrities known for being inspiring and positive. I know a few who have their off days, maybe angry and focused on what's not working, and in that emotional state they are not their most powerful selves. I myself have had seasons where I focus on all the evidence of what's going wrong, and when you are focused on what's going wrong you start to *believe* what you see, and you start believing that "that's it," like looking through a knot hole in a fence. You start seeing and believing *just that piece* and you don't see everything else. In emotions we get myopic. We can get myopic in a great way, or in an awful way.

Everyone has moments when they do both, or when they do either. Even high-powered executives have off days, get myopic, and have to confront, "How do I get out of this?" Donald Trump has moments. Jack Welch, Lee Iacocca—I don't care who it is, they all have moments in which things don't work. Some of them have learned the skill, though—Tony Robbins and Donald Trump are great examples. They know how to shake it off, shift their physiology, shift their focus, and shift their beliefs. Some people train themselves to do it quicker, so it doesn't last, so it doesn't grip them, so they don't go through five years of failure!

THE DIFFERENCE

A *great* example is Martha Stewart. She got thrown into prison for heaven's sake, to be made an example of, for insider trading. Now she could have, and I'm sure she had, some very negative moments. "This is not where I want my life going," and so on. But she very quickly shifted her focus. She decided to create *three* television programs. She had one program when she went in, she had *three* when she came out! She also started another magazine! Her focus, her self-talk, her beliefs, turned everything into "How can I benefit from this? How can this be great? How can this be a wonderful opportunity?" And I'll tell you what, not everybody does that. She took it like, "Okay, this is going to be my retreat time where I . . ."—not that that's a fun place to have a retreat but she made it out to be—"I'm going to use this." I mean, nobody has ever talked about it again. In fact most people have completely forgotten that segment and I honestly admire the *heck* out of her choices. Seriously. I can't even tell you. I don't know whether she did or she didn't commit the crime, and it's not my job to judge, but how she utilized that time and how she did not succumb was amazing. She *could* have said, "That's it, I'm over, I'm done." But that's not what happened, not at all. In fact quite the reverse.

Successful people can lose it all and get it back. Donald Trump lost it all in the 1980s. When you have that—and he definitely has moments when he's negative, he's pissed off and has what I call *un-resourceful emotions*—and all the guys at the top have them: Tony Robbins, the late Steve Jobs. The difference is *they know unconsciously how to do this,* how to shake it off, change their physiology, change their focus, use their self-talk, change their beliefs, and change the *meaning* and make it work. That's the difference.

Many people are familiar with one or two of these things but not the whole package found in the Five Star Formula. They can do affirmations all day long, but if they have not also changed their physiology, they have not changed anything. If you change your physiology and you still believe all the lousy stuff, guess what? You're gonna get it! So these factors definitely work together. And we each have our own pattern. I have clients who start with focus. I personally start with physiology. I've got clients that start with their self-talk. As a coach, I utilize what they tend to start with first, and I help them shift all the other four. And guess what? They've got a whole new way of being, a whole new emotional state.

BUILDING HABITS

It can be like putting on a magic coat that gives your client new abilities, but they have to put it on each day and practice wearing it. If they've got all this old stuff, if they've been doing this old emotional state for any duration, it won't leave overnight. It's a habit, and like any habit, it's going to take 21 days to change it. To actually shift into a new gear takes another 21 days.

We all have a core fiber, a bent we are born with, but the things we learn are the *habits* we have. And I believe while we do all have the *ability* to access all of the emotions, we do come with personal bents. Some of us are extroverts, for example. And there are personalities that are going to lean more on the side of cheerful, happy, optimistic emotions, and there are personalities that are going to lean more in the introspective, analytical, calm side—not necessarily dark, but skeptical and hence more negative emotions. This doesn't mean they're stuck in any of these unless they've made it their habit, however. They have all of the ability to do any emotion, and whichever personality they are, they can practice the spectrum of emotions.

If you look at the text *Power vs. Force*, by David Hawkins, there is a whole list of emotions, the top being *joy*. With the four personalities, the sanguine, the high-I will be more on the spectrum of joy in nature, but it doesn't mean you won't see somebody with that personality who gets completely angry or completely apathetic because they have all the ability to exhibit any of them. I will say that the melancholy or what we would call in the DISC model the high-C personality, is more analytical and skeptical because they're analyzing and deconstructing things by nature. They can lean more towards the sadder, more down emotions, but the melancholy has complete capability of being in and experiencing joy. All of these personalities need to choose what's going to help them to get where they want to go. They need to practice it and make the emotions serve them. They need to make it a *habit*. That's really what it boils down to. And none of us are locked into being in a certain emotion.

We are born with *none* of the five elements in the Five Star Formula as fixed things. You're not born with belief. You're not born with a propensity to focus on something. You're not born with physiology. You're not born with meaning. What we do is mirror and match the people who are around us: our parents, our siblings, our teachers, our mentors, our coaches. We learn all of that from these people and model it. But we're not born with any of that.

In fact, in *Power vs. Force* David Hawkins has actually calibrated and measured the vibrational wavelengths for the various emotions. Highest is Joy, apathy is lowest. He's done lots of work and he's still with us. Stanford and other research institutes are doing lots of studies on these things. The people there who have done the happiness studies have certainly done more of the research around this work but *Power vs. Force* is a great book—hefty to get through initially but fascinating. And it does talk about the calibration. Maybe one need not know particular wavelengths and so on but I do think it's important for us all to know that every emotion does have a different effect. What Hawkins was noticing is that, just like with playing a piano, if you hit a C, all the other Cs vibrate. You want your client to be where all the other positive energies are vibrating and where their energy is best operating.

Another phenomenal book I have every client read which is more of a layman's version of *Power vs. Force* is by a lady named Lynn Grabhorn, called *Excuse Me, Your Life is Waiting*. Even if you only read the first three chapters, it's a great and valuable read. I make every client read it because this gives a third party endorsement about how important the emotion you're in really is and what effect your emotions will have on your results. Super important. Yet some have doubts, like those high-D alpha achievers. They might think, "Oh, let's skip over that. I don't need any of that stuff. Let's just make the plan and get going towards the $5 million dollar contract." And they're doing it from *anger* and frustration, and overwhelm, and this whole state is where their vibration is lousy, and they wonder why nothing is going right! It's funny but it isn't funny! This subject is really important.

I do get clients in a perfectly awesome state and they don't need to start there, with emotion. However, I will say that along the way this gets covered for everyone at some point, in my coaching. I get clients that are so excited about coaching and they're so excited about specific targets they are wanting to go after and we start going after them and it's all awesome and wonderful. Then they have a week where all the wheels fall off, and they access that awful place where nothing's working. And it's good to know that we have the power to shift that, and voila! The wheels start going back on.

One fellow who was reluctant to bring his nervous teenager to a therapist explained he did not want to enable a victim mindset in his child. Perhaps he's overly concerned but it's actually one reason I personally got out of therapy! And therapy is where I started. I had my degree in movement psychology and was an adjunctive therapist in an acute psychiatric facility. I was charting alongside the psychiatrists and everyone else so I was privy to what the psychiatrists were writing. I was thinking, "Oh my gosh, these people are just normal, neurotic people that need help, need hope, need focus, need to shift." And if I had the knowledge then that I have now with this, the Five Star Formula, I would have been in there revolutionizing because honestly, those people need to have their world cracked.

And the labels, the identity piece that something is wrong with you, and the whole connotation of having therapy, while there are reasons to have psychiatrists and psychologists to get people out of what they're in, whether it's abuse or something else, can be very useful. But at that point I think there is a space for a *coach* to take over and move them into the future. I don't think that psychologists are very equipped to do a very good job with that. It's nothing wrong with them as people, it's just that their focus has for so long been analyzing what's wrong and why it went wrong. But we've just seen what focusing on that does! If you focus on what's wrong and why it's wrong and what happened, *you're going to get more of it! You do get what you focus on!*

One of the things I'll cover in this book is that law of focus and I'll tell you, you do get what you focus on. What you focus on enlarges and becomes part of you. That's a universal law, like the law of a vacuum, like the law of gravity—not something I came up with at all. God created that! If I tell you to look around the room focusing on everything that's blue and then to close your eyes and tell me everything that's blue, you can do that. If I then ask you to tell me what's brown, well, you weren't focusing on that. It's the law of focus. The more you focus on something the more you have beliefs around it, the more you make it mean stuff, and it will take you into whatever kind of emotional state it takes you to.

We have here, then, with this information and the Five Star Formula, all you need to move a client from an assessment of who they are and who they need to be, into real change and real habits, habits that will guide them straight into the future they have dreamed of. They simply need a little help from a coach to get there.

KEY 5: EXECUTE AND IMPLEMENT

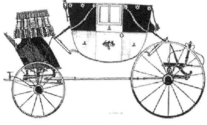

A Neat Ornamented, or Town Coach.

I USE THE *TARGET PLAN* every day. It's a philosophy, it's a way of thinking, and it's actually the way I chunk everything in my life, to be honest. I have gotten so accustomed over the last thirty years of operating like this that today I don't hold an appointment, I don't get on the phone (except for playing with my grandson)—there's really no longer anything I do where I don't have in mind, "What's the hoped-for outcome from this meeting? What's

183

the outcome I have in mind for the time I have on this phone call? What's the thing I want to come away with? What's the target I have for my business?" When I was first starting this book with my editor, my questions were, "Okay, what do we want this to do? What is the end result going to be? What do we want to go away with at the end?" It's always the first thing.

And here's the thing most people skim over because they think—they kind of sense—they know why they're doing stuff, but I just ask them, "Have you ever set a goal (or a New Year's resolution) that you didn't achieve?" The answer is always yes. Every person says yes and that includes me and everyone else. I then ask, "Are there things that seemed inconceivable that you did in fact achieve, maybe shockingly? Was there a guy or girl in your life that you really wanted and now you're married? Maybe early on it was 'Oh my gosh, she's the unachievable girl—I would love to have her in my life,' and in fact you made it happen?" We all have things in our lives like that as well.

The reason those things happen is we have enough motive. We actually get leverage on ourselves to do that. So it's important to have leverage. And if you've got enough reasons why, if you've got enough motive, if there's enough cost or pain involved in not having it happen, believe me, you will ultimately figure out how to get there. The *how* will unfold.

That's the philosophy of target planning:

1. It's first of all knowing what you're after, knowing what the target is.
2. The second part is having lots of reasons why.
3. The third aspect is *how* are we going to get there? What are all the options? Then let's pick the best of those options to actually get that target.

Fifteen years ago I sat with one of my very best friends and actually did this on a fluorescent green—I'll never forget it, it was actually a fluorescent green three by five index card—at a restaurant. We created a mattress company. The company went on to produce *millions* and become a top-producing mattress company. She has since sold it and moved on to doing other things in her life but it's interesting because this philosophy can go with you as you move on to other pursuits. You can move on to using it for setting up large companies or you can actually put together a simple little party. It can be something huge or it can be something teeny.

I do this for every single category in my life and I do this with my clients. I take every part of their life—usually we start with the one that is chomping at their heels. Where the fire is closest to the fence, we start there. I'll give examples in a moment but the first thing I always do is teach them the template for the Target Plan.

THE TARGET PLAN

Dynamic Life Target Planning

Target/Objective_____ Date when_____

Menu of Options	Motive, Leverage & Reasons Why
	Categories of Questions

Menu of Options

1. How can I make this target happen?

   What are **ALL** the things I **COULD** do to achieve this target?

   (Answer this until there are no additional answers.)

   By when?

   _____

   _____

   _____

   _____

   _____

   _____

   _____

   _____

   _____

   _____

2. Asterisk (•) the 20% that will most likely achieve 80% of the result.
3. Schedule the 20% items.
4. Review weekly and update.

Motive, Leverage & Reasons Why
Categories of Questions

1. Why is this Target a must? Why is it important?

2. What will...this target give me?
   ...it allow me to do?
   ...I gain if I achieve this?

3. What will...it cost if I do not achieve this?
   ...I lose?
   ...I not be able to do?

4. How will I feel when I have hit the target?
   What will it mean to me?

Dynamic Life – Cynthia Freeman – PO Box 1001 – Newport Beach, CA 92659 – (949) 642-7200

Sample Target Plan Form

Knowledge isn't power, it's potential power.
Execution trumps knowledge any day of the week.
—TONY ROBBINS

STEP ONE

Get out a piece of paper. Draw a horizontal line across, about three inches from the top if you're using an eight and a half by eleven inch sheet. Now split the bottom part in two with a vertical line, so you now have two columns underneath that top section. Now draw, as big as you can in that top section, a circle. That's the *target*. This is the *what* and the *when*. The first question to answer is, "What do you want *specifically*," and circle the word *specifically*. Your client has to be able to measure and monitor this. They have a servo-mechanism inside their brain that is going to steer them and guide them towards something specific, and I find that if the target is fluffy, it's problematic.

For example, I might have a client say, "I want to be *happy*." I have no clue how to define that. If it is not definable, if it isn't measurable, they're never going to attain it! So what I have them do is define what it would look like, how it would feel, how it will be different, make it quantifiable. The next question, then, in this same circle, is

188

"By when?" Without a timeline or with a "whenever" on this, it will never happen. "I'm going to get married *someday*. I'm going to write a book *someday*. I'm going to create a business *someday*." Not gonna happen. If there's no urgency, there's no push, there's certainly no motive to make it happen. It's going to happen "sometime" in the future, "out there." It's not real. It's sort of a wish, to be honest.

This is the whole first part of the Target Plan. Simple, uncomplicated. Don't try to put every category or everything all together. Separate it all out.

STEP TWO

Your client now has the two columns, representing the two railways or roads to get to their target in the circle above. "I'm going from San Francisco to New York." Notice I didn't say "I'm going *east*." That's that sluffy, sloppy, "Let's be *happy*," sort of thing. You're going to make sure they've got a very specific destination. You're going to have a timeframe for when they're going to get there. And these two railroad tracks on the bottom of the page are going to take them there.

On the right-hand side you'll have all the reasons why. You've got the *what* and the *when* in the circle at the top—the target—and the reasons *why* are in this right-hand column.

Another word for this is "motive," hence, motivation. I cannot count how many times I have had clients come to me and say, "I need you to motivate me. I need to get motivated." And what's awesome is that because I know about this Target Plan, I immediately know they are trying to achieve something without anything in this right-hand column. I immediately know what's missing. I immediately know all I have to do is ask them questions and get them in this right-hand column. They will then have motives and drive. It gives you motivation. It gives you leverage—the *oomph* to move forward. It's what I call "the drivers," which are all in this right-hand column.

There are four categories of questions. These are not the only questions, but I find these are the four categories of questions that I ask to get to this target. In the first category the questions might look like this:

- "Why is this result or target a must?"
- "Why must I create this business?"
- "Why must I get married?"
- "Why must I have a family?"
- "Why must I write a book?"
- "Why must I weigh x-amount of pounds?"
- "Why is it a must?"

I have my client underline the word "must," because if it ain't a must, it ain't never gonna happen. How many New Year's resolutions have never gotten accomplished? It's because they weren't a must. They were, "You know, if it happens that will be fine. If it happens that would be great." No, no, no.

Writing this book, for example, for me became a *must*. I was driven, I was motivated to get it done. We can ask why something is a must for a client, or for myself, but it all comes down to, "Why is it important to me? Why do I want to achieve this? Why am I *driven* to make this happen?" And it's quite interesting that your client can ask what is essentially the same question in five different ways and they will get five different answers. In one question, the client might get stuck and might not have an answer quickly. For example, I might ask, "Why is it a must?" And they say nothing. I then ask, "Okay, why is it important to you? Why are you absolutely driven to do this?" and they might then have 49 answers!

The second category of questions are along the lines of, "What will this target or goal, *give you*?" In other words:

- "What's the upside if you achieve it?"
- "What will achieving this target allow you to do?"

- "What doors will it open for you?"
- "Who will it allow you to meet?"
- "Where will it allow you to go?"
- "What will it do for you?"
- "What is the upside?"

And conversely, with an upside figured out there has to be a downside, and that's the third category of questions:

- "What will it cost you if you do not achieve this?"

It's amazing how motivated by cost people really are. I just went through this with a client on the phone. It was really interesting, and she knew it, too. She said, "Oh no, here we go, it's the *cost*. If I don't do this it will be death. If I don't make this happen I honestly don't know how my family will be fed. I don't know how I'll survive. Honestly."

It all depends on the client. You'll find some clients are going to be more inclined to move *toward* something and some clients are going to be moving *away* from something, from the cost, for example. So what's the cost if your client doesn't achieve this target? Other ways of asking that are:

- "What doors will be closed?"

- "What will that not allow you to do?"
- "Where will you never be able to go?"
- "Who will you never meet?"
- "What will you never know?"

They're all different facets of the same question.

The fourth category is engaging your visceral reaction, asking:

- "How will it feel when you achieve this?"
- "What will it feel like?"
- "How will your life look?"
- "What will it mean in your life if you've done this?"

Once my client has gotten enough leverage and answered a lot of these questions, I go through with them and get at least ten answers in each category, because with 40 reasons why—and there's nothing sacred about the number 40, but with *lots* of reasons why—there's going to be *something* in that list that is monumental and highly motivating. At the end of this time I ask, "Out of every reason you've given me, what are the one or two things that really *grip* you, you know, viscerally, and just compel you, drive you, push you, pulls you and drags you to that result to make it happen, no matter what—no matter what you're going to make it happen?

And while it's different for everyone, they *always* have a response. For some, like one gal, after giving me all the polite reasons for losing weight before going to a reunion, as an example, told me "Well, for my children, and so on." But if I would have guessed I would have said she probably wanted to look great for all of those ex-boyfriends that she had, or all of the cool kids she wanted to look really good for. And while all of those might have been motivating reasons, none turned out to be *the* most motivating reason. The most motivating reason was her mother-in-law had told her she would never get back into shape, that she would always be heavy after she had her two children.

She didn't get to that answer for a while. It came out in the cost category of questions, and it must have been number thirty-five on the list, but when she hit it you could tell—the bells rang, and that was it! Two months later she was way ahead of schedule. She was at her target weight. She was looking spectacular and hadn't missed a day at the gym *ever*. So the importance of finding the right motivation is critical.

STEP THREE

The third part of the Target Plan is getting there. Santa is not coming down the chimney to give your client what he or she wants. They're going to have to go into action. And the key is to go into the *right* action, not just any pitsy, diddly, piece of action. In the left-hand column I call this a "Menu of Options." I have my clients brainstorm and really answer the question, which is asked until there are no more answers. "What are ALL"—and I have them capitalize and circle the word *all*—"the things you <u>COULD</u>"—I have them capitalize, underline and circle the word *could*—"do to achieve this outcome that you've set for yourself?"

Then they start brainstorming, and I do not let them edit. I encourage them to get out of their head whatever comes to mind. I liken it to being in line at the salad bar and grabbing those spring-loaded salad plates: every time you take one off, the next one pops up. You want them to get to the bottom of that stack, where the icy-cold plate is. That's the object. If they don't get things out of their brain and put onto the list, thoughts keep spinning around up there and they're in the way. They need to get them out of their head, onto to the paper. The point is they're not going to do everything on the list. This is not—and I capitalize, underscore *not*—a "To Do" list. This is a "Could Do" list.

Let's say your client has 40 ideas about how they're going to get slim and trim, reach their health and vitality target goal of 120 pounds and wearing a size four (if they're a woman) or 180 pounds with a 32-inch waist (if they're a man). Whatever their target is, it's specific, it's measurable, they've got a timeline on it, and they've got all the reasons why they want to hit it. Now they're going to brainstorm a list with maybe even 100 things they could do to get to the target.

Then look at the list, and put Pareto's Principle into play—that is, the "80-20" rule. Most people on this planet are out busy ticking the list and doing all the 80 percent things that only give you 20 percent results. They're busy just ticking boxes and trying to do stuff, just getting stuff "out of the way," and it's about just go, go, go. They lose sight of the result. They lose sight of the target. They lose sight of what they actually want to make happen. They get so consumed with the list of stuff that they're doing all the wrong actions and not getting the results. So you want your client to look at this list and decide, "What's the 20 percent I can do to give me 80 percent of the results?"

Let's say they have a list of 40 things. Well, roughly eight are going to stand out, and if they do those eight things they'll get so close to the result that the momentum will carry them the rest of the way. And that's something we actually find with Pareto's Principle. By the time they hit 80 percent they've got so much momentum and such a big win that one of two things happens: either they've got so much momentum that it doesn't take much effort to do the last two or three things to complete it or 80 percent is good enough! Eighty percent might be close enough that they're happy with it. Now, true confession: if they're looking for a husband or wife, 80 percent is not good enough. *But,* in a lot of cases, 80 percent is close enough, right?

They then take those 20-percent items and schedule those in their calendar. And here's the magic of what happens. If they have done this process, if they've sketched each part of a target plan for each part of their life that they need to focus on, guess what happens? All that's scheduled are the right actions, the 20-percent actions that are going to give them results, and all that they are doing is showing up for their schedule every single day. They don't have to futz around with a bunch of different lists. They don't have to worry about "I didn't get 79 things done today." All they're going to do are the things you have scheduled. You should be able to look at their schedule—and I say this to my clients all the time—and you should be able to know that any particular item is the *right* action for one of the key targets that they have. What I find with my clients, and this is where the Five Star Formula and all the things that we transform in the Five Star Formula comes in very handy. If they start getting off track and not doing the things that get the 80 percent of results and they're not seeing progress, then what we find is one of two things:

1. It could be they don't have enough motive, so I go to the right-hand column with their reasons why.

Remember it takes both tracks to get there. From San Francisco to New York, they need all four tires lined up to get there.

2. Or it could be they are not doing the 20 percent "right" actions.

So it's really simple to look at this. And it's super easy to do one of these for each of the things that are important in your client's life. I have a target for family, I have a target for my business. As I write this sentence, I have a target for my book. I have a target for my health and vitality. I have a target for travel and leisure. Those are samples. I have one of these Target Plans for each of those areas and in a given day I see to them.

I spent time with my grandson and my daughter this morning. That was awesome, and that's associated with that target for family. I've spent time working on my book today, writing this chapter. I will spend time coaching people this morning and this afternoon. Later on I will be talking to a friend and we'll be firming up our plans for a trip. This afternoon I will also do my daily three-mile hike for an hour for my health and vitality. Those are 20 percent actions to get the 80 percent of the results. That describes the actions in my day. Each one of my actions are attached to an outcome, to a target that I have.

And this often makes execution and implementation a breeze, but we're not quite finished, not yet. It gets even more fun.

KEY 6: INTEGRATE AND CELEBRATE

A Neat Ornamented, 12 Price Coach

ONCE YOU'VE GOTTEN THROUGH the CREATE-IT process to the point that your client is actually executing strategies, the next phase is to *integrate* and *celebrate*. They've now got new tools, new strategies, and they're implementing this all inside of a plan that they've created, so they've got very specific targets they're aimed at. You then help them integrate that into their life and into their practice of their daily life, into the areas of their life they are working on, be it growing and expanding their business or their team, developing a new business, or maybe improving their health and fitness so they have more time to work on their business. It might be in their relationships—it applies to whatever areas they're working on. Now after they've integrated it all in and it's part of what they're up to, there is celebration. And celebration is really as simple as "let's rehearse success." Key Six of my coaching method then, is to integrate and celebrate.

We talk often about going to the next level. We've talked about the Wheel of Life, and using that as a sort of assessment of where the client currently is. What's interesting is that by integrating, you find out how critical it is to celebrate *everything, big and small*. This very thing has come up three times in three coaching calls I've had the day of writing this. You have to notice every small motion going towards targets. We call these "small wins." Every time your client has made progress, small or big, you can look back over the last week or the last summer, the last season, last year, and you can see that they have moved closer to their targets, closer to the things they said they wanted. We want to celebrate them all.

How and Why to Celebrate

And by celebrating, we mean having your client stand up, cheer, physically pat him or herself on the back, and say, "Yes! yes!" with a power move and excitement. Every single time they do that they *anchor*, they remind their body of what it feels like to win, what it feels like to have success. Success breeds success. And remember, I talked about the Law of Focus, right? Well if a person is always focused on fixing things, on solutions, then what they're focusing on there, is what's *wrong*, and they're not celebrating anything. If they're spending most of their time just saying, "Okay, I did that!" and they check the box and move on, asking themselves, "What do I need to do better? What do I need to fix? What do I need to do next?" -- if there's no celebration, it means all their focus is on what's *not* working, what needs to be improved, and what's not there yet. The focus is on what's empty—on the *empty* space. And guess what? The Law of Focus will kick in and they're going to find they get more of what they're focusing on, which in this case is that empty space—which is what's wrong. It's not that you don't work on those things, but you want to celebrate, you want to focus on all the progress, you want to focus on little progress, medium progress, and huge progress. You want to celebrate and anchor in *winning* success, every single time they have even a tiny piece of that. Every time I have a section of this book done, I'm going, "Yes! I finished that section! Yes!" I'm celebrating because I'm making progress and I'm focusing on winning. I'm focusing on the success and I'm building on that success." Again, success breeds success. I'm anchoring in the memory of what success is and what success feels like.

I wonder what life would be like if every parent and grandparent celebrated every single time a child or a young adult did something even remotely in the right direction. I know we do it when they're very young: the moment they start to crawl, we're cheering. The moment they start to walk or to run, we are cheering. The moment they have success (or even near-success!) in potty training, we are cheering! So somewhere along the line we kind of forget to do that and we don't help the child. Now you, the *parent,* may be cheering, but are you helping that *child* cheer? Are you helping your spouse to celebrate and cheer? Are you building the habit of success and winning all around you and in yourself? So it's really important to integrate and celebrate all of those wins because it builds the muscle for more success.

There are lots of ways to celebrate. It doesn't have to be complicated, either. In fact it can be very simple. I have my clients stand up where they are. I make them drop everything, I make them put their fists in the air and say, "Yes! Yes! Yes!" I have them cheer. You can have them jump up and down, you can run around the block, you can light a sparkler and twirl it around and say, "Yes! I did that!" Whatever little celebration they might like. In fact I want you to decide right now, what's your way of celebrating? Not putting it off—but celebrating right now all of your success? (I think that sparkler idea is a really good one. I was thinking fireworks would be even better, if a little bit "out there.")

THE SUCCESS FORMULA

Very often people begin to have success and they start to move a wheel out towards the tens (if the center is zero, meaning they're not good at all in that area of our life, and ten means it could not get any better). If they're starting to see that things are working, if they're starting to notice that they've moved their wheel out into the eights and the nines, and then the ten region, it is time to write down what they are doing that is their winning formula. I guarantee you—and I've been coaching now for 25 years—that we're all going to have more hiccups in our roads. So when it is all going great, when it is all working, when your client feels like, "Gee, I don't have a thing to work on right now, my life is spectacular!" That's the moment to stop and celebrate, to write down, "What is your Five Star Formula?"

When they're in their success, what's the formula? What is the recipe that they're running? Because *that* is what's causing the success. What is their focus? What are their beliefs? What are they saying to him or herself? How are they walking? How are they talking? How are they breathing? What's their facial expression? What are they doing that is causing all of this, and what does it mean when they are doing this? *Write it down!*

I cannot tell you how many coaching clients have come to me a couple of years after the fact and said to me, "Oh my gosh—you had me write down my success formula. That day when I said I didn't need coaching, and I didn't have anything to work on, we wrote down my success formula, and I tell you what, I just went through a month of absolute dumps! Nothing went right. I pulled that out and I swear to you, that's what turned me around! I put that success formula on. I shifted my focus, I shifted how I walk, I shifted how I talk, I shifted what I was thinking about, I shifted what I believed, I shifted what I said to myself, and guess what? Things started to turn around. Things in my relationship started to work. Things at work started to work—I *did* make the sales! Things started to happen in a great way, and I'm back on the road again. It's not smooth sailing, but I tell you what, without that I'm not sure how many months or even years I would have been in the dumps!"

So it's important to capture when it's really working, to capture how it's working and what those winning formulas are because they will help your client win again.

And, hooray! We're on to Step Seven!

KEY 7: TAKE NEXT STEPS

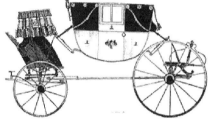

A Neat Ornamented or Town Coach

MOST SCHOOLS OMIT CRITICAL final steps, and this is the reason they get "good" results. Others get ridiculous, off-the-chart results, and then sustain their wins. When your client does achieve their goal, it's time to move the goal posts. What was a "10" just hours ago is your new "5." Their standards can get higher and your game bigger or better in any number of ways. So, in Step 7, the Seventh Key of the Coaching Process is what I like to call "Next Steps," because it's all about redefining the target, taking Next Steps, and focusing forward. In fact, this is what the word "coach" actually means. "Coaches" are carriages, and even football coaches, life coaches, and executive coaches are carrying. It's about carrying someone who really can't do it themselves because they have blind spots.

So, you've gone through this whole process of creating a relationship and exploring and examining and accessing where they're at. Then you've gone through transforming and doing all this coaching and shifting and expanding and growing and strategizing. Then you've gone into execution so now you're implementing all those ideas and tools and strategies. And you're doing this inside of a plan that they've created so that you've got a very specific target that they're aimed at. Then you integrate that into their life and into their practice and into the areas of their life that they are working, be it their business or their team, or be it improving their health and fitness (so that you have more time to do that business!) or be it in their relationships.

Coaching applies to all of that. And after you've integrated it in and it's part of what they're up to, there's celebration. And celebration is nothing more than "Let's rehearse success!" So now you've had success and you're still celebrating that, but here's the key: most people—in fact most coaches—stop there. That's where the program ends. I get these achiever executives and they go, "Now what?" They go, "Uh, okay, is that all there is? Is that it? Okay, I've arrived. Now what? I'm not thrilled. I'm not happy. I'm not fulfilled." They don't label it in any of those ways. They just have this feeling of "is that it?" And it's usually because the only way you can really guarantee success is by really focusing forward and having what's next. "What's next" can look like designing an exciting, fulfilling retirement. "What's next" can be orchestrating to sell a company, or it can be next level. "What's next" can be "Wow!" I hear people all the time, using that phrase "going to the next level." Well, what does it mean?

TEN IS THE NEW FIVE

For me, what it means, if I've gotten to this place and on the Wheel of Life everything is nines and tens, like "Wow! I'm hitting it out of the park—it couldn't get any better—this is sensational," it means life isn't done. For you and your client, this means they're not done and they certainly don't want to go into the ho-hum-ness of life. You don't want them to go into boring homeostasis because if you allow that and you don't design next steps and the next level, here's what happens: I can't tell you how many clients start sabotaging all of their wins. They start suspecting something can go wrong. They start doubting and worrying that it can't be this good, so they sabotage the relationship. They sabotage the success at business. They sabotage their weight loss or their fitness targets. They start to do this because they can't believe they could possibly live at ten and they have to have some place to go to.

So what happens is they design challenges and problems to solve. Executives and achievers are brilliant at this. I cannot tell you how many people I've watched who have to go back to square one or near square one and solve the problem all over again. I've done it myself. Here's what I do instead, as a coach, and that's why there's this seventh step. It's called "Next Steps" to guarantee success and really build consistent momentum. What it is, you've hit nine or ten in your relationships and in your business or with your team or with your earnings or your health. I did this with a company when I realized that they were going to sabotage things: I told them, "Okay, this is the new *five*. In other words, this is your new baseline. This is your new medium. You're no longer at a nine or a ten. This is now a five. So if this is five for your earnings, what would a ten be? If this is five in your relationships, where you are, then what would ten look like? How would you experience that? If this is a new five, this is the new baseline for your health, so what would a ten be in your health? You get the idea.

So, this is how you determine and define the next level. So the assignment for your client, if you they have reached a very high nine verging onto a ten in any part of their life, any part of their business, in their marketing, in their systems, in their staff, in their team, in their earnings, or in their sales, I would actually say, "This is the new five. And if this is a five, what would the new ten be?"

This is a great way to be looking forward into the new year. Now, they may have an area that is not a nine. Maybe they worked really hard to get from a three to a six! Alright, that's fine. They're still working on that, and you could ask them, "What is the ten? If you're at a three, what is the ten?" You go back into these transformation questions. You go back and ask, "Okay, what's preventing you from getting to ten? What's standing in the way? What do you need to transform?" All those coaching questions that you asked back in previous chapters you can reevaluate, but notice that it doesn't really stop. I have clients that I've had for eight years, for example, and they left me for three years and now they're back again, because they understand that the minute all the wheels are rolling forward they need to actually capture what's working. They need to capture how it is working so that they can grab their recipe for success to repeat it. They realize if they're having all that success and they're at a nine or a ten, that it's now the time to say, "Okay, that's the new five.

Now what would a ten be?" and really set a new Target Plan in place for that new ten. You redefine the target and you get leverage for *why*—if you know the steps, *why* it's a must to get there. Ask what it will give them, what it will cost them if they don't, how it will feel and what it will mean to them when they've arrived there. And then, what are all the things they can do to achieve the new target, that next level, the new direction that they're going?

You know, it's really important to remember that we all want results. Your clients really, really, really want results— it's what they are with you for! The reason they show up is because they expect you to reveal to them what's stopping them. And they expect you to help influence them in getting to their target, to help them with tools and strategies to get to that target. So really, what you do is you both conspire together to get to that target and now as you've completed those seven steps, you now begin those seven steps again to go to the new level, and you conspire together to really create that next level.

PUTTING IT ALL TOGETHER

Remember the Seven Steps, or the Seven Keys of Coaching, and that they make the acronym, "CREATE IT":

1. **C**reate

   Relationship
2. **E**xplore
3. **A**ssess
4. **T**ransform
5. **E**xecute

6. **I**ntegrate & Celebrate
7. **T**ake Next Steps

So really, in putting it all together, you start the process again. The first piece is you go back and create that relationship again, because without relationship coaching does not work. A coach is someone who's going to help co-create that future. You're going to be a sounding board. You're going to be someone who will ask great questions so they think of new ideas and possibilities. You're going to open up the doors and the windows so that they see other opportunities. But you, the coach, are not the solution. You do this is in what some people call a co-active relation. You conspire together to make this happen.

The second step of this is that then, after you have a relationship and after you've developed this safe space to be in, you're going to explore what it is they really want. Where are the dreams? What's stopping them? What's preventing them? You're going to explore and examine all of those pieces that I mentioned earlier in this book. Where are they, really, now? And you reevaluate where they now want to go. What are their needs? What are their values? What are their beliefs? What do they think their obstacles are? What are the hurdles they need to get over? What is helping them? What are their strengths? And what is stopping them? And then of course, you want to assess. I love doing this through tools and little assessments, but certainly, you can do it through questioning such as, "Where are you now? What's keeping you there? What are your strengths? What are your limitations? What do we need to build on? And what do we need to diminish?"

My favorite coaching question is, "If you could, what would you expand, grow, change, shift, or eliminate?" And then, going into the next phase of this, once they have decided where they want to go, and where they are, you're going to start to do transformation. You're going to use a Five Star Formula to remind them of the emotional state, and who they need to be, and create that identity that's going to get them to the new level, to the new result of where they want to go, to get them to the target. That's going to be kind of their armor that they're going to wear to get them to where they want. And then of course, they're going to have a plan, and that's when they get into execution. They're going to execute strategies. They're going to have a very clear and monitor-able (yes that's a word, I made up) target that they're going to get leverage and by that I mean just *why* it's a must. What is going to drive them? What's going to compel them absolutely, without anything stopping them, so that they achieve the target, so that they stay in the game, so that they know exactly where to get back on the rails if they get derailed? And then, they're going to integrate those changes into their life.

It might look like putting new things into their schedule. It's going to look like new habits. It's going to look like new rituals. You're going to integrate and celebrate—and I did say *celebrate*. You're going to integrate it and then you're going to celebrate like nobody's business. You're going to celebrate the smallest, tiniest, littlest progress in the forward motion because you are going to build their success muscle. You are, instead of focusing on what they don't want, going to focus forward on what they do want and you're going to build and build and build on that, and yes, in the meantime, you're going to diminish and demolish and eliminate and eradicate the stuff that's not working. They're going to dust it behind them. And of course, they're going to take next steps.

You're going to look at whether they've succeeded. If they've achieved their targets, you're going to absolutely set new targets, you're going to make that the new baseline. That's going to be what I call the new five, and they're going to go to a new ten, and they're going to hit it out of the ballpark once again and they're going to move in that, they're going to carry themselves in that forward direction.

The Target Plan really is the key strategy that I love to use because when a person has got leverage on him or herself, they've got momentum in it. They're only doing those actions that I call the "right actions," that are the purposeful, attentive actions. They're doing that 20 percent that's going to give them 80 percent of the results, that give them momentum to carry it through to the end so that they can see progress all the time consistently. And, they're not going to waste time doing a bunch of stuff knowing that the goal in life isn't to be busy.

THE GOAL IN LIFE

The goal in life is to get down to business and to really have a life of fulfillment, as I see it. That target is going to help your client achieve it all and juggle everything. When I had a very successful real estate career, I believe people asked me for advice because honestly, I was a single mom and they couldn't figure out how I was able to date, go on vacations, work in my kids' school every Friday, and spend time with my kids in the evening. How did that all work? How *could* it work? They didn't get it. How could that all happen and I could still do all of these real estate transactions and still keep to business? How could I do all of that? The truth is I had a Target Plan. I was only doing the 20 percent that was going to give me 80 percent of the results and I wasn't therefore wasting a lot of time. I aligned my values and I had strong beliefs moving forward, including a belief that it was possible.

So, I'm here to say that it *is* possible, and that your client can put this all together. Besides having a Target Plan, another key is them having an identity that really backs up their target. They've set those targets and they've determined who they say they are in their identity, and when they say, "I am this," and, "I'm not that," it is consistent to that person who's going to go towards that target and achieve it. And it's as simple as doing the Five Star Formula. That will take them to the being they need to be. I know it's cliché, how people say, "We're not human doings, we're human beings," and I would ask, "Who are you being?" Look at your Five Star Formula and ask, "Okay, what's your emotional state?" Are you being courageous, bold, and kind and generous? The combination of those emotions will take a person in a really different direction than if they're somebody who's frustrated and angry and stingy and in scarcity.

Isn't it?

So who are they being? And is that being going to take them to your goal? Because that's their guarantee of getting there.

The only limit to your impact is your imagination and your commitment.

—TONY ROBBINS

GET YOUR FREE BONUS!

In appreciation of your buying and reading this book, and as an encouragement of your success as a coach and in your life, please accept these free bonuses I have arranged for you.

Visit this page today!

http://www.cynthiafreeman.com/get-your-free-bonus/

PART 3: POWERFUL COACHING SESSIONS

SEVEN STEPS

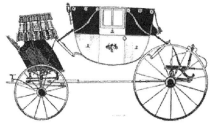

THERE ARE SEVEN STEPS to a powerful coaching session. One session is typically one half hour or hour-long phone call, and all these things occur during it:

1. Connect
2. Check In
3. Celebrate Wins
4. Clarify

5. Coach Using Strategies
6. Create a Plan of Action
7. Condition & Commit

I have found in my coaching that there are many versions of this, that there are lots of schools of thought as far as what elements need to be part of a coaching call to have it be productive, to have it get results, and to have it be impactful. You want to have *impact,* you want to inspire, you want to get results and you want your clients to come out on the other side really remembering what happened. And I will say that some calls are this way and some calls aren't this way. When I hear a coaching call and these elements are all there, it's funny because I can guarantee there's a result that happened in that call. There is a client on the other side of that call who is really impacted. Usually that client will come back the next week or in a month or two and say, "Oh, remember when we did a-b-c? I've been doing this and this and this." It's funny because those are the calls in which all of these seven steps occurred.

STEP 1: CONNECT

The first step in the seven steps is that you really want to connect with your client. Now that sounds like it happens obviously, but I'm going to confess: I have personally been involved in calls and I have listened to calls where the coach glosses over this step and there is a disconnect. By that, I mean that there is no rapport, and it comes out later in the call when the client says something like, "No, that's not what I meant. I wanted to go this direction." But they're usually too polite to say anything right away and usually the client will disclose this 25 minutes into a 30-minute call. The client will say, "I have a question today," and the coach has gone off and covered some completely other topic or thing that they presumed was the issue or the focus or where the client "should go," and in fact they didn't really stop and connect with the client and get into rapport with them.

We talked earlier in the book about getting rapport and different methods to get into rapport, but certainly asking questions is one way. You really want to relate to who they are, where are they, how are they doing, and so on. You want to (not literally) take their temperature and score the client as to where they are from zero to ten—you know, "one" being that they are really funky, the wheels have fallen off, not doing great – to ten, when you have to peel them off the ceiling. I don't do that but I will tell you what I do: I do "take their temperature," and by that I mean I have listened to the physiology of their voice; I have listened to a couple of the things they're saying, and then I—at the top of the page where I take notes, and I do take notes on all my clients—actually make a note of where I think they are. Are they a "one?" Are they a "five?" Are they a "two" or an "eight?" It's interesting because then at the end of the call I can say, if they were a "two," did we get to an "eight" or "nine?" If they were a "ten" have we maintained that and are they ready to go to the next level? I think that's important.

Again, I don't sit there and score the client. I've listened to calls where people who are coaches do it, and it sounds like ticking boxes. I don't like that. I want it to sound organic, I want it to sound natural. So just for me I'm making, on the coaching side, a mental note, and I do, by the way, always make notes on my clients.

STEP 2: CHECK IN

The second step in that powerful coaching call is to really check in. I have heard entire calls not get started for 30 minutes because they were checking in, and they were checking on "how is life, how are the kids, how's the family?" That's all great, grand, and wonderful, but only if the client has brought it up. However that's not coaching. If you'll just check in when I say you should be checking in you'll be okay. I have also found clients that reported on a coach and were furious because the coach never checks to see if they've done anything with what they talked about last week or in the last coaching call. So what this *check-in* is about is, what is working in their coaching? Did they find the coaching useful? Did they apply what they learned? If there was a strategy or a skill or a tool or an "a-ha!" did they use it? Did they notice it? Did they pay attention to it? Did they work on the actions of the plan that the coach and the client set in place?

I also check in on *what worked?* What worked in what you did? What progress did you make? I also check in and say, "Okay, what were the hurdles? Where were obstacles? What didn't work? I then make a note (and I don't go into deep discussion here as this is where a lot of coaches go off on a tangent, where as I said earlier they're not fully in rapport because they're not on the topic, necessarily) on where the client wants to go. The client may have come with something they really want to work on.

It is important to make notes to keep the continuity of the coaching. It is important to check in on these things and anything in which they had obstacles. With anything that didn't work, I make a note and in a moment I come back to it or make a note for another session. I'll make a note on the impact—I'll ask questions around the impact or what happened because of something. I make notes and then I automatically go right into any baby step. I then go right into the third step, which is celebrating the wins.

STEP 3: CELEBRATE WINS

Now this does not mean they arrived at the end goal. This means they have made a step—maybe even a half-step— forward. Even if they had three steps that went backwards, you want to notice any forward motion towards their target. We want to celebrate any progress—anything that was a piece of a win—that was made toward any targets they may have set.

The reason it is so important to do this is because we are mostly, as a human species, in the habit of noticing what's wrong, about beating ourselves up about what didn't work, about noticing where the wheels fell off. And I'm not saying you are to ignore that, you certainly do need to notice that, but you really want to take hold of what's working to be really celebrating what's working because it develops a new habit. If your client gets in the habit of winning, if they get in the habit of looking at what's great, if they get in the habit of success, it's going to lead to more success. It's going to lead to more winning. I am going to talk about the law of focus, and let's be clear: what a person focuses on will grow and expand.

What a person focuses on they ultimately will become. So it's really critical to realize that if they're focusing on what went right and on the wins, they're going to have more of the wins. As a coach you're a cheerleader and you're cheering for them. You're giving them a clap and virtual high-five and that's awesome, but the truth is they don't need *you* cheering. What they need is to get in the habit of *them* cheering on their win, so I will have a client high-five themselves! I will have the client raise their hand in the air, bend their elbow, and pat themselves on the back. I will have the client get up out of their seat, jump up and down for joy, do the big fat happy dance, and go crazy for ten seconds so that they really notice "Yes! I did something right!" Because goodness we certainly know how to focus on what's wrong.

Let's say the coaching call is 30 minutes. These first three steps—connect, check-in, and celebrate the wins—is about five minutes. This is not going on and on and on. I know it's taken pages to describe all this, but this is a five minute piece of a 30-minute session, to do all three of those.

STEP 4: CLARIFY

Then the fourth step happens and we want to *clarify* the outcome. Based on the target that they've set that they are aimed at, based on the progress that they've made or didn't make, you want to then clarify the outcome of the call. In the first couple of calls it may be that they're actually setting the targets for the quarter or the year or the next three years.

They may be developing a whole complete life plan, but what you're doing here is working on an area of their life. Let's say it's their health and vitality, or their business outcome. Or you're going to start with your relationship outcome; or you're going to start with the financial outcome—whatever area of focus you decide on for this call or session is the plan you will get in place so that they can begin to take an action on that.

So it's important to really clarify and get clear on the outcome. It's also important to keep referring to this outcome throughout the call and that's going to help your client to stay on target. Now a lot of clients will encounter things that will pop up in the call that may lead them off target. It's like shiny pennies, they start chasing them on the call. And in a 30-minute call you are not going to slay an army. You're not going to achieve every outcome on the planet in one call. Coaching is a process. Coaching is something that's going to happen over time. And so if a client brings up a bunch of things that they want to do or they start to see a shiny penny and go, "Oh, we need to work on that," and let's say there's 20 minutes left in the call, I will ask them, "Would you like to put a pause button on working on the outcome we've been working on that we set for this call, and do you want to shift gears or would you like to park this for now?" (I always have a parking lot for future outcomes.) "Would you like to park that and come back to it next week or in our future calls?" I won't forget. I've got a giant four-by-six-inch Post-It that's sitting there where I have "Parked Outcome," so I don't forget that I want to come back to those pieces. And sometimes the client, depending how pressing it is, will say, "Let's work on it." Sometimes the client will say, "No, I do want to work on that but we need to get this other thing done first."

Now sometimes you've been working on things and you just continue to work on the next phase of what your client has been making progress with. Great. That's a perfect outcome to be working on. You note the progress they've made and it might be time to add a new area of focus. You might open a crack in a new window so to speak or it may be something that might have shown up during the check-in that you've made a note on, and the client may say, "You know I do want to work on that but I've had this challenge come up with my spouse," or, "I've had this challenge come up with my child," or, "I don't know what to do, I'm just running rampant with my credit card," or, "I really need strategies around how to work with this boss and what to do with my team."

So they've had a new situation come up and it's more important that they get that thing out of their lives, on a plan, working on it, or off their mind because until they do they really can't focus on anything else. So I always come with an agenda to a call, an outcome for the call, but it's never my agenda or my outcome over the client's. If the client comes with a different outcome then I just park my agenda and we work on their outcome that day and we know where we're going with it.

STEP 5: COACH USING STRATEGIES

The *fifth step*, once you've set the outcome of where you're working to go today and you've set it clearly so that you know whether you're on track or not (and keep reminding the client and keep coming back to that outcome throughout the call), you then really want to coach using the coaching strategies that we have. There are dozens of schools of thought around coaching. There's what is called "coactive coaching," there's "directive coaching," "results coaching," and everybody has their own spin on what the strategies might be. For the sake of simplicity here, one of the things that I will say on the first level, is, "Is the outcome of an emotional or an internal nature, or is the outcome that we've set, is it really a target or achievement oriented outcome that we have set?" That will tell me which direction I need to go first.

If it is an emotional, internal, needs, values, or identity outcome, those are all *internal* outcomes. If it's an internal outcome I will immediately go to the Five Star Formula and we will begin working through it and give them an assignment to establish that. I might do an identity exercise. I might do a whole needs evaluation and I might do a values elicitation. I might do all of those during the call to be able to work on an internal outcome.

I will do a Target Plan and really get to the meat of what the clear bull's-eye is for their target if it's an achievement thing. Maybe they need to hit a number at work or they need to hit a target for their health and vitality or they need to hit a target for reducing debt or they need to hit a target for making more money. Great, then do a Target Plan. I'm going to make sure that they have absolutely enough leverage and enough motivators that they are driven and compelled to make it happen. And then we're going to go through and create an action plan that's based on the 80/20 rule where really the only things in their diary, the only things on their agenda are those 20 percent action items that are going to get them 80 percent of the result. I'll start there and see how the progress goes. Then no matter what direction the client is going in, we absolutely are going to create a plan of action.

STEP 6: CREATE A PLAN OF ACTION

Now, the plan of action is going to be related to what you've just worked on. So if your client has created a Target Plan it's pretty simple. They are going to commit and they are going to do those 20 percent actions. They are going to put it in their schedule. It's going to be Thursday at two p.m. It's going to be Friday at nine a.m. They are going to have specific times. I might even get them to be accountable to me. They'll send me text messages or emails. It's not anything where there is a conversation. They just say, "Did it! It's done! I talked to x number of people. I made x number of calls. I talked to the team. I had that conversation with my wife."

It might be these internal pieces: "I rehearsed my identity statement twice today," or "While I was rebounding for 20 minutes this morning I practiced my new, empowering emotions." So they might record that and have times when they are rehearsing these things where they become conscious to that. So you want to set the target of what they are able to visualize. What does success look like? In taking what they worked on today and putting it into action, what does that look like? Together you set that target. You make sure that they've got reasons they want to hit that, reasons like leverage on themselves to actually have success in this. Then you make sure they schedule those key actions.

STEP 7: CONDITION AND COMMIT

With whatever it is that they have decided they have got to do, they now need to condition and commit. Conditioning can look like rehearsing these internal items or it can look like putting it in the schedule *now* and taking action *now* so that it is absolutely *in*. They make a commitment to themselves and to you, the coach, which is actually in their schedule so there is no skating on this. When they've created the action and they're really committed to that, you absolutely want to condition in what the value is that they're taking from the call. You want to condition the value of the call. That way they know you've made a note and in case they trip up, in case they have challenges, you can come back and say, "Well, you told me that this was really important *because* . . . You told me it was valuable *because* . . ." and you get them realigned. Situations in life and circumstances happen. Sometimes it's our job as a coach to really remind them of why they're in this for the bigger scheme of things, for the bigger win, when little challenges hit them.

And those are the seven steps to a powerful coaching session or call:

1. Connect

2. Check In

3. Celebrate Wins

4. Clarify

5. Coach Using Strategies

6. Create a Plan of Action

7. Condition & Commit

GET YOUR FREE BONUS!

In appreciation of your buying and reading this book, and as an encouragement of your success as a coach and in your life, please accept these free bonuses I have arranged for you.

Visit this page today!

http://www.cynthiafreeman.com/get-your-free-bonus/

PART 4: BUILDING A BUSINESS

BUILDING YOUR BRAND

A Neat Ornamented, or Town Coach

AS WE'RE NOW DISCUSSING building a business, one of the key pieces is building a *brand*. To have a brand it is important to develop a unique factor and to have some point of difference—whether it is a visual point, or a talking point, or a niche point—but some point of difference. It's important that everything you do is consistent, whether you're out speaking, whether you are writing an article, or whether you are blogging. If you are doing anything at all you want it all to be congruent and consistent with your brand.

Another piece is that you really want to become a specialist in whatever it is your brand is all about. For example, you might be a specialist at doing a certain assessment tool and be known for that, or it might be that you are a specialist in a niche and that is what people come to you for. And really what it becomes is that you actually develop fans, what we will call *raving fans* that want you or want that/your brand. People do select things based on the brand. Any time you promote yourself, you want to lead with whatever that brand is.

YOUR BRAND IS YOUR PROMISE

Now something of a bold statement, yet true, is to say your brand is your promise. And I'll use some examples. Let's take McDonald's golden arches. I'll never forget seeing them in Amsterdam when I was 20 years old and had been traveling through Europe for three months. I had traveled by plane, train, automobile, bus, metro, and every other form of transportation, and Amsterdam was my last stop before flying home to the United States. It was there where the first McDonald's had been built in Europe. Today I would not be so excited about seeing those golden arches or eating those hamburgers and fries but back then I was so excited about something that was like home. It was recognizable, and I knew what I was going to get. I knew what the sauce was going to taste like, I knew the brand to the nth degree,. I knew there would be no surprise in the product and so I waited for an hour to get a Big Mac and fries. And here's the thing: it was *exactly* how mine at home, in Fullerton, California, tasted, and *that* is a brand. It is completely and totally consistent.

For everyone who talks about brands, one of their favorite stories, and mine too, is that of Coca-Cola. I don't care what country you're in, in the entire world, there doesn't have to be one word—I don't have to understand any of the language, but if I look at the shape of the bottle I know that it's Coke. I actually have a Coke bottle that I got in Israel when I got married in the 1980s. It's a glass Coke bottle with that recognizable shape, and it's scripted. I know what it says because the script goes in the same scrolling script as Coca-Cola, but it's in Hebrew which goes backwards. I mean, think about it, right? Hebrew goes from right to left and not left to right. But I still know that it says Coca-Cola. So the brand is a promise. Everyone who knows Coke expects a certain taste, expects a certain pop with that soda, with that kind of bite that goes almost up to your nostrils when you first taste it. I have to confess I don't drink sodas anymore and I haven't for years and years, but I know what that taste is like.

The most high-profile branding mistake in history was when Coca-Cola decided to bring out New Coke, because even though they wanted to broaden who they were, that was not the brand. Anyone who knows marketing, anyone who does branding, know that this was the most miserable, quintessential failure of all time. They went against what everyone around the globe knew, when they were (and are) the most recognized brand on the planet, at least as of this moment. When you've done so much to develop a brand, are you going to please everyone? No. But, are you going to make your raving fans happy because you are consistent and people know what they are going to get? Absolutely. So when you are thinking about who you are going to be, you want to build your brand, and build a brand made on a promise.

Your brand is a promise. You want to develop fans around that brand. They have expectations and they fall in love. They will trust you, and if you change anything, you lose the trust. So the goal in all marketing—and especially in today's internet marketing—is for people to know, like and trust you. Note those three words: know, like, and trust. That's what a brand is all about. It says that I am trustworthy, I am consistent. The goal is to develop strong loyalty. So it's about having a strong identity that backs your promise.

Here's another branching example: I have a nose for green umbrellas. My energy can feel out and find a green umbrella. Hello Starbuck -- very globally and completely consistent, thank God! I would have been highly disappointed otherwise because I happen to be a coffee connoisseur. I love the fact that I can find a green umbrella and that my Americano is the same in Singapore, Sydney, Australia, New York, and in Newport Beach. It doesn't matter where I am, I can find the same coffee and have it under the same green umbrella. That's a brand. It's really the delivery on that promise, right?

PLAN YOUR BRAND

Now that we've discussed what a brand is and how it's important, you have to know that a brand is *planned*. You can't just willy-nilly hope that a brand is going to arrive. Now some people get lucky. They decide they are something, they have a tag line, and they develop some sort of a following. They get lucky and they develop a brand by accident. I've used McDonald's as an example, I've used Coca-Cola as an example, but if you look at what Madison Avenue does, and you look at cosmetics like Olay, and you look at L'Oreal, which is a huge, international product, each of those has a brand that is very specifically planned.

Do they change? Yes. They may change greatly over time. For example, you will see that the colors will morph. The logo might morph. The tag line might shift and change a bit, but they never change everything at once. They change one small thing at a time and they plan it and they change it strategically over time, so that literally, I can't remember what L'Oreal looked like 25 years ago, but I can tell you their tag line, the coloring, their logo, has completely shifted over those years. But because they've done it one small piece at a time and very strategically, they are able to shift them very gradually, becoming something, sometimes, totally different, but without losing their identity too quickly. That is the strategy of how to change a brand, and the most important piece here is that you actually plan your brand.

An Entire Experience

Some people think a brand is a logo, and even here I've used McDonald's and Coca-Cola, which are very visual examples, but a brand is way more than a look. It's about look and color—I'm going to a seminar this weekend and I guarantee you the gal will have a purple dress on because her look has been that from the beginning—but the truth is that's not the brand. The brand is that she has a niche, the brand is that she has a tribe following her with raving fans, and the fact of the matter is that people come to expect that she is very natural, very authentic, that Lisa is a real straight shooter. You know what's coming. You know what to expect. You have a certain expectation of what she is actually going to give you.

And there are other strong images that people know that need no explanation. Here's a great example: If I show you an icon of an apple with a bite taken out of it, you know what it represents. Does it represent a food? Absolutely not. Does it represent a computer? Not necessarily. It's a perfect branding example, just like the Nike swoosh. Those are perfect examples where there is a strong visual but they represent an entire field. There's an expectation. I know I'm going to get awesome service. I know everything is going to be consistent with Apple. I know that, for example, with Nike, that there is an energetic, vivacious, comfort, and it can be athletic wear now for all seasons. So it's not just running shoes anymore, it's an entire experience if you're talking about Nike. And with Apple, it is an entire experience. They have become not all things to everyone but all kinds of things to all kinds of people, and it is actually an entire experience.

I think that's what you need to look at with your brand. Whether it is a company that you're thinking of, or whether it is coaching direction, or whether it is really just about anything you decide you want to do, you want to make sure that everything is congruent, everything is cohesive, and you actually plan the brand and you decide from start to finish what the promise is you're making, what the feeling is you are wanting your audience to get.

I have been speaking at seminars a lot lately and people, even before they have met me or seen me, just from hearing about me, are starting to tell me all the same things about me. In other words, from seeing me speak, from seeing my videos or website, from other ways, it seems my brand is consistent. I am a completely straight shooter. I am really direct. What you see is what you're going to get. I am not pulling any punches, I am giving out a real, clear message and I am going to give honest feedback. You are going to get information about your blind spots, and you're going to get clarity and perspective. There's not going to be any fluff and you're going to learn how to really complete projects, get results, and be able to dance with all the areas of your life but you're going to eliminate all the extraneous. That came through, funny enough, in both seminars I gave last weekend, totally different people, totally different seminars. Who I was described as being is that person, and here's what's fun: I realize that I am developing a promise. I am developing a *brand.*

And now it's my job to make sure that every single aspect of what I'm about is consistent with that message, that if I am about no fluff, if I am about being a straight shooter, I have to make sure that the images that I portray on my website, in my marketing pieces, in my blog, are consistent with this message.

YOUR BRAND ONLINE

In this day and age whatever your brand is (and it's not about your letterhead or your business cards anymore although I certainly would have them be consistent with your brand), it's very, very, very, critically important that you do have an online presence. Now I don't know what's coming in 20 years so it may be that there's a brand-new flavor of the "oh-my-gosh." Believe it or not I was born before the internet so there was a day when we didn't have online anything. Here are a few things to make sure that your brand online has the same consistency:

FEEL

First of all, you have to think about what you want people to feel, about what promise you want to make to your tribe of raving fans. And in this you want to make sure of a few things. This all comes under the heading of "branding," yet might not be pieces you would ordinarily think about. So first of all what do you want your identity to be inside this brand?

Who do you want people to say that you are? I think that's really important. And it's important to work out what is the attitude of your brand? Are you edgy? Are you direct? Are you nice? Are you spiritual? Are you romantic? What's the flavor? That goes hand in hand with the emotion, with the tone. Your brand will actually have a tone, a flavor, a behavior, or an emotion to it, and that's the *identity* to your brand.

NICHE

Then you want to make sure that you're not trying to be all things to all people. You know what they say—when you try to be all things to all people you become "nothing to nobody." Poor English, but true. It's very important. The more clear your identity is, the more "niched" you are, the easier you are going to be to find on the internet. And it's very critical that you make yourself easy to find.

INSPIRATION

One of the things in your branding process is to go out and ask yourself, "What do I like?" Find what is consistent to who you are. The title of this book, for example, *The Power of Done*, fits perfectly with my professional brand. It's clear, articulate, direct, short, like a punch, it's consistent with what everyone said I was. So it's going to be easy to find, easy for people to navigate to me.

You want to steal good ideas! You want to go out and see looks, colors, designs. Of course you're not going to actually copy trade names or plagiarize, but if there is something you really love, if something is working, then go out and grab it. If it expresses who you are then it's important that you use that. Again, you want to have a clear identity and you want to be easily found and that comes with that clarity. Don't hesitate to go out and combine two or three things that come together. In my case with the design of this book, I looked at other covers, other designs, other tag lines, colors, and so on. Start to find and tweak things that express who you are.

As you are designing what your brand is all about, you want to pay attention to your competition. What is their brand? What's their promise? It doesn't mean you can't promise the same thing, but how can you do it in your own unique way, even if you're offering the same thing? Maybe, if you look at your competition, you will spot something missing. Maybe there is a gap you can fill. And to be honest, there are lots of men in coaching that offer something similar to what I do, but I think as a woman I offer something unique in that I am very direct. I shoot from the hip and really give perspective that most women want to dance around, be nice and playful and fun and be fluffy. So I think that's a gap that I fill. Just an example.

BEING HUMAN

One thing that is really important is you want to make sure, unless you are selling caskets, that you do not take yourself so seriously that the message is boring and dead. You want to make sure there's a life to this and that your brand has an authenticity. I don't know any human on the planet that doesn't laugh at some things, and certainly the best thing to laugh at is yourself. I think it's important because you are trying to relate and "grab the eyeballs" of human beings and not robots (although I realize robots will find you as well, a la Google), but mostly what you are aimed at is other humans. So if you are not human, if you don't appear to have a real, authentic, vulnerable appeal, you're not going to grab those eyeballs. So it's important to look at the lighter side of life.

MARKETING CHANNELS & CONSISTENCY

The other piece is you want to remember all of the marketing channels. Now I'm not going to name them all here, let's be clear, so this is certainly not the end-all-be-all. I remember the day when there was just one online service called AOL. Then there was EarthLink. Now, where are all of those today? So obviously if I mention names those are going to morph and change. You're going to want to go with all of those that are current out there. But you really truly do want to have a brand consistency, a message that's out there, about who you are, in every platform that's out there.

With some channels you will find it harder than with others. If you're business-oriented, you're going to want to work LinkedIn more. If you are in information and in coaching you want to have a Facebook presence. How to actually use these in marketing will be addressed elsewhere, but you want to be kind of everywhere. You also want to have an email presence. I would say these days you want to have a blog presence. We happen to be in a time where videos are the most current thing—in fact YouTube is one of the most searched sites. So if you don't have videos out there you're sort of lost.

But now we have print, personality, videos—so how do you make sure you're consistent with all of that? You want o make sure that your style is the style you're marketing yourself with on LinkedIn, on Facebook, in other places. You want to make sure that the image you are using on your web page, your blog post, or in videos on YouTube, you want to make sure that the feeling you are giving, that the promise you are delivering is the same everywhere. Just like my example of being in Amsterdam as a kid. I was so excited to buy a five dollar hamburger over there when they were just one dollar in the States. There was a promise I was banking on. There was a feeling I was going to get—I was going to feel like I was at home, and being a kid in Europe for three months, I kind of had a streak of home sickness. You want people to have a certain experience of you, whether you are appearing in writing or in video, or anything in-between.

INDIVIDUALS ARE VISIONARIES

The brand has an emotional solution, it has a visual solution, there is a verbiage solution, and when you're diagnosing your brand you want all of those components, and that equals brand clarity. Take New Coke, for example. People want variety, right? Well, the truth is people *don't* want variety. They devised the New Coke and it bombed. Henry Ford has a quote:

"If I had asked people what they wanted,
they would have said faster horses."

Right? People don't realize what they need and what your brand should offer is that next thing, out on the edge. If you ask people what they want they're going to go with the status quo and they're going to be like the people around Henry Ford—they're going to want faster horses. And what he offered was more quickly built, horseless carriages. You don't ask the people because they are stuck in the status quo. As a mass, they are not visionary. Individuals are visionary, and I think it's important to mention, do *not* ask your friends and family what your brand ought to be! Now this group I mentioned earlier gave me their impression of me, but I felt completely at home, completely endorsed, completely in agreement that they described how I believe my brand is. I didn't ask permission and I didn't ask anybody what they thought I should be. People en masse can be stupid. Individuals alone can be visionary.

PERSONAL NAMES AND BRANDS

It's really important to realize that even when people use his or her name as a brand, the person himself is not the brand. It's the whole promise, the whole experience that's actually the brand. Tony Robbins for example, *he* is not the brand,. But his name in print -- the set of words "Tony Robbins" -- has come to represent a promise in which you know what you're going to get. You know if you go and see Tony Robbins you're going to have a certain kind of experience.

You know you're going to have a peak performance experience that's like a rock concert but with words. You know what's going to be delivered. What's interesting is, it's the whole package. Donald Trump is another example. It's a whole experience. Now notice, he's done real estate development and television shows, and all of it is consistent with the upper echelon and upper crust, with total flair. It's all consistent with the promise he is going to give you.

There is Bobbi Brown makeup. The brand is not *her*. She's got her name on it, it's all very specific, but she's not the brand. The brand is cosmetics, a cosmetic experience, how you're going to feel, you're going to be healthy and young with vitality. There is a promise that's with this, and that's what the brand is. I just want to make this clear because people can get confused as to what a brand is.

I would say you really want to think hard about whether you want your name to be your brand. There is a restaurant called Crosby's and I know he doesn't own it, but there is a whole experience that goes with it—you know, that kind of cushy atmosphere and so on. Take Jennifer Lopez. She made an industry out of her brand and companies will go to her to buy that experience. Another is Sarah Jessica Parker. Jessica Simpson has done this as well with shoes and design. Elizabeth Taylor absolutely did this and Madonna is another one. All of them represent different things. Jessica Simpson is spunky, young, fun, playful, cute and flashy. Jennifer Lopez is sexy. Madonna is power and total perfection, delivering on the highest level. They've got movies, music, blog posts, Twitter, all of these mediums and they all need to be consistent. And that's why each is a brand. That's why we know them as a brand because they don't do anything inconsistent with their brand. It doesn't matter whether they are actually there with the product or experience, or not, the brand stands.

BRAND EXERCISES

Stop for a moment and think about your favorite brand. What is it you love about that brand? Ask yourself if your brand should be along those lines, then, if that's what you love. And is your business customer-focused or is it customer-driven? Your customers determine the business (which does not mean you go ask your friends and family what to do), so be sure your business is focused on your actual customers and driven by them. They have to feel they are served. Your customers need to feel that they are benefited and that they are valued.

After you've done the exercise of thinking about your favorite brand and considering what they are delivering and what they are all about, and because you want to achieve your own brand clarity, make a list of what you give your customers. For me, for example, I give them energy, direction, strategy, clarity, and perspective. Those are examples of what I know I give. You want to make sure that whatever these four of five things are you are giving come through in your materials. Does my business card give off energy, direction, and so on? Does my website give that?

And along with what you give your customers, you should ask yourself if all your platforms give these things. What do you do that motivates people to purchase? You want to make sure your materials make them want you, even if you're a non-profit and you're free. Do you encourage people to purchase and to come on board? Do they want to be a part of your tribe? In fact here is something you'll want to test yourself on: I've got customers who signed up for two and a half years of coaching because they didn't want to lose me. Do you have customers that would be upset if you shut shop? Really and truly, would they be upset? If so, this is an indicator that you are going in the right direction. As you plan your brand you want to ask yourself where you want your business to go and you want to grow through those phases and stages. So you want to be thinking about your goals for three years from now, five years from now, and where your brand will be. Where do you want the brand to go?

Now here is something funny. I use Coke as an example a lot because it's the most well-known brand in the world. You can go to the middle of the most secluded village in Africa and they know Coke. But with a brand that is successful, people will get upset if that brand shuts shop because people feel they own that brand. And truly, you want your tribe to own it—not own you, see, that's not the brand. The brand is bigger than you. You want your tribe to really feel like they own it, like it's theirs. This is their domain and that's because you are really serving them at every front.

YOUR MISSION

You want to be sure as you think about your brand, to ask yourself what you stand for. This is also called a mission statement. My mission, really truly is: "Through coaching, whether it's online, person-to-person, or at the front of a room, I offer straight-up, no-holds-barred clarity and perspective. I really give people strategies to get things done, and to be able to do some of everything, to eliminate the extraneous, eliminate the distractions and to get people to where they really want to say "I was part of that. I accomplished that."

And I really think that is so important. I have a client who can say he has been at all of his daughter's rowing

261

regattas, at every one of his son's basketball games, at all of the water polo games, and also closed the biggest deals of his company's life, and celebrated his 30th wedding anniversary. He has learned how to get away from the fluff, away from the time wasters and the shiny pennies that are the distractions and get to the results that count, and do some of everything. So I would ask people what their mission is.

You want to start by deciding what your end goals are and get going in that direction, right? You want to make sure that you protect that. You can change like brands – which change over years -- but (if they survive) they change strategically. All the parts of a brand's appearance do not change at once. They might change the color one year, and then morph more through the years. Maybe the colors are red and orange starting out and they have a goal to get to black, so they might start adding in black and then gold. Eventually they are black and gold, but it was done strategically.

On color, you do want your color to say what you want it to say. My colors should be strong colors like blue and black, for example. Studying other brands and images is always helpful. Ask yourself what they say to you, what you like and don't like about them. Look at icons that you like. Symbols that are out there. Then ask yourself which ones represent what you are about. This is about consistency so choose well. You want to look at shapes first, colors, second, and content third, when designing a logo. There are a zillion people and places out there to get affordable work done on a logo, freelancers and so on, but have an idea ahead of time.

Divide and Conquer

Now as far as how much you should follow your heart versus following your market research, the old "art for art's sake" thing, first of all they hopefully dovetail together. Beyond that, I'm not going to judge anyone for making a buck. But if you share from the heart it will strike a chord. It will actually reach your audience on at least three levels, depending on your brand's strength.

It should be three things:

(a) It should be memorable
(b) It should inspire brand evangelism so that people will want to belong to your tribe
(c) Dependency: where someone is fully engaged with your brand and they look to you to fill their needs and wants.

So you can sell without heart, and you can reverse engineer, knowing what people want, but if it isn't congruent with your brand, you do not want it under your brand heading. It dilutes your brand. Then it will actually split your brand or make your brand more diverse, which confuses your audience so that they don't know what you are or what your brand is, and you destroy the brand. This is why people will publish under pseudonyms, for example, so they don't dilute or confuse other brands (in this case authors). So if you are working on a brand and building a brand, you want to do all you can to stay consistent with that brand.

But I'm not going to judge. If you want to write trashy love novels—and there is, by the way, another "Cynthia Freeman" in the U.K. who writes such novels, who is hugely known—the same rules apply. In fact this other Cynthia, to her credit, has a very consistent, recognizable brand! She's like Barbara Cartland, the English romance novelist often seen in her signature pink outfits—total brand, and consistent with that brand. Barbara Cartland would walk out on to a TV interview and she would be in a beautiful, probably thousand-dollar negligee with fur around the collar, the whole flowing robe, it would be satin or chiffon or whatever. She was true to her brand and it would be soft, beautiful pink. Pink roses to the side, white and pink everywhere. One hundred percent consistent with her brand.

Suzanne Somers is a brilliant scientist by nature. She played a ditsy character on *Three's Company*, a stereotype which she couldn't get out of for the longest time. And today she writes books on health and wellness and is a brilliant marketer to boot, but it took a long time for her to morph. You do choose your brand. In fact you have to choose. And I would not do "all of the above" under one name. If you want to go off and make your mint by reverse engineering, and just give the people what they want, with whatever sells like hotcakes, for example, then you should do that under one name and seek out a brand built on your heart and intellectual passions under another. One can ruin the other if combined. But I don't want to judge people. I am not the judge.

YOUR BRAND AND YOUR NICHE

When we say a brand is a promise, in actuality it will probably be a promise to a certain niche, not just to everybody everywhere. One of the things that you want to get very specific about is who you are speaking to. As a coach, you can go to CoachFederation.org, which is the International Coach Federation website, and you can actually look at the myriad of coaching niches that there are. That's not the end-all-be-all list, but that's certainly a great start of, *where could I have a niche?* There are whole niches for ADHD, there's a whole niche for women in divorce, and so on. I don't know what your thing is, but you want to have your brand really be specific to the niche.

YOUR AVATAR

A great way to specify your niche is to create an avatar. It's so critical to know who your avatar is—in other words, your ideal client, your ideal employee, your ideal colleague or whoever it is who you are coaching. You want to get very, very specific as to who the person is, so that every piece of text, blog writing, copywriting, subject line and video content are all geared to that person. There are lots of ways to arrive at an avatar but here's the thing: in your mind's eye when you're developing your avatar you want to ask yourself who this person is and what it is that they love. What do they hate? What do they believe? Where do they shop? Where do they live? What programs do they listen to on the radio? Which radio station do they listen to? What do they do in their spare time? What television programs do they watch? What kind of movies do they go to? What would they never go to? What kind of car do they drive? What brand of clothes do they wear?

All of these pieces end up summarizing the person that you are writing to, the person you want to attract. You're going to ask questions that delve into such specifics as, Do they have a family? Are they married? Are they single? How old are they? Where do they go to school? Did they go to school? What kind of jobs might they have? I could go on and on with a selection of questions you might have for this person, but truly, you want to answer as many questions as possible so you know exactly what this person is thinking, what they believe, what their aspirations are, what their frustrations are. And I recommend that you actually journal -- actually write pages -- about this person so you know everything about them.

Here is one of the assignments I have given a lot of my business clients who need to have a clear idea of their avatar and be clear about their niche before they *ever* think about marketing (otherwise they will give mixed messages in their marketing and it will go in every direction). I will ask them, "Can you think of four or five people that represent this group and ask questions about them?" What's important is your clear perception of these people and how they think and what they believe. The clearer you are, the better. Then you can go into doing your marketing.

YOUR ELEVATOR PITCH

After you've gotten crystal clear about this you are starting to develop your brand. Now you begin to know about those people and you can begin to make a promise, or build a brand to that niche, that avatar. After you've done that you really want to create what we fondly call in the industry your "elevator pitch." It's not that you're always selling things, but let's face it, people ask you what you do. You ought to have in one sentence who you help, how you help them, and what benefits and results they get when you've helped them.

That should all be in one line, one sentence. For example, "I help executives who have plates spinning and falling off the sticks to actually get them all spinning in unison and get results and get things done." That's what I do. That's my elevator pitch. It's a one-liner. Most people say that's not enough detail but here's the thing: if you've got an elevator pitch that's sexy enough, that hooks them enough, they are going to want to know more. So then you elaborate and you tell them a little bit more about how you work and what options you might have.

For example, I have an option in which a client can meet me over the phone two or three times a month for the following six, eight, or twelve months. I've also got a program in which a client can meet me over the phone like an "all you can eat" buffet: they might talk to me three or four times in a month, maybe three times in a week, and then twice in a month. It will vary but it's there when they need it. I have another option that is two full days—really it's a year's worth of coaching—and after two full days they walk away with a complete blueprint of how to operate their life. With the actual right actions in their schedule when they leave, they know exactly what they're going to do the next day. That's how it works.

That was a three-minute version of my elevator pitch. You've got the 30-second version, the three-minute version, the four-minute version, and then you've got the "Wow, I'd really love to meet with you and find out how that works," version, which might be a 20-minute meeting in which you go into a little bit more detail and they decide whether they want to work with you or not.

So it all starts with you knowing your avatar. You can't create an accurate elevator pitch or a three-minute elaboration on how you work if you don't know specifically who it's geared towards. This is really critical in your branding. And just a few logistics: you want to make sure that you've got a really accurate website that speaks to your avatar, speaks to that market that you want to go after, and attracts the people who you are interested in. Have professional photos taken, as well as a professional video made. Have something that definitely represents you and something that your particular audience would love to have.

A TRIBE FOR LIFE

So now I've covered what identity for your brand is, the emotion you want your tribe to feel and if you are causing them to want to be a part of it. You've thought about what your mission is inside that brand, and that all of this needs to be congruent across your brand. What is important? What are your values? Are all of your statements everywhere congruent? Your values, your mission, your identity, and being congruent on all those fronts creates a brand that people know, like and trust and it creates a tribe for life so that they feel they own the brand.

LOGISTICS OF A COACH

A Neat Ornamented, or Town Coach.

T O KEEP YOUR SANITY together you want to have *systems* in place. I have found this to be true time and time again—in fact I found this to be the core of my success in my previous career in real estate. For most people, like big businesses, having systems is what causes them to be effective and efficient—and profitable, for that matter. Coaches are, unfortunately, often very much like real estate agents, in that they kind of treat their occupation like a hobby rather than a business. But if you want this to be a business, if you want this to be hugely profitable—and that is absolutely do-able—it is critical that you have systems in place. This is how you make yourself effective and efficient: by having systems for how you are able to track things, able to hold on to things, and able to file things (electronically or with paper). For all of the above and more, it's important that you have systems.

Welcome Pack

Right off the bat, you want to come up with a welcome pack. This can look like an intake folder, or this can be in other forms. I received a welcome pack from one of my very first coaches, in fact. I was trading coaching when I first got into the business because I wanted to be coached and she needed to coach. We were both experimenting with what we were putting together and her welcome package was beautiful.

She had folders made. She had assessments inside one of the flaps. She had a welcome letter. She had a questionnaire. She had a sample of a call prep sheet, which had the rules of the game or guidelines as to how we would operate in there. And that was really great that she explained how it was going to work, and who was responsible for what. She had an entire information sheet so she knew all about me, including my family and birthdays, anniversaries, and all of that sort of thing. Today your welcome pack can be paper or it can be electronic. In fact I have a complete welcome pack that is electronic. It includes personality assessments. It includes links to love languages and the PQ assessment. I also have a complete information sheet. I have a "rules of the game" sheet. I have a questionnaire in there, too, so there's all of those pieces. Here's what you need to ask yourself: in order for you to do a spectacular job with your client, what do you want to know about them? You'll want to include that. What would help you with your coaching? What would help you be the best coach ever? So that's what you want to have in your welcome pack.

QUESTIONNAIRES

One of the key pieces of a welcome pack is the questionnaire. In fact, if I didn't have them fill out anything else and only wanted one piece of information, I would want the questionnaire filled out. I've helped coaches around the world, literally, formulate their questionnaires, and here's what I say to them: "First of all, who is your client? Do you have an avatar that you're working with? Are you working with empty nest women? Are you working with alpha male executives?" I've got one coach whose questionnaires I helped develop and he is working with miners (as in coal) in

Australia, so he has a very, very, different client. So ask yourself, what do you really want to know about your client? I had some coaches who had 50 questions on a five-page questionnaire. By the time they got it back, it was 50 pages because their clients had to type in their answers and it just kept expanding. I've taken questionnaires and I've seen lots of questionnaires. They can be very effective with only five questions—five key questions of things that are critical to your person. The key things that you would want to know about a client, or employee, would include:

- What are the three key things that they want to accomplish? And out of those three, what's the driving one that they absolutely must get results in?

- The second and probably most critical thing that I would want to know is where they feel they have won or accomplished before. What are their top three accomplishments that have happened in their life? What do they want for number four?

- And then I would ask, "What was it about you, or what was it that caused that to be a success?" See, I want to know what they think helps them to win. I want to get a clue as to what their winning formula in the past has been because I might be able to use that. That might give me a good insight.

- Another thing that I might want to know is what would be helpful. How would they most like to be coached? This is going to start to tell me whether we're going to be a great fit, how to get leverage on them, and what style is going to work with them.

Now, sometimes I don't fully believe my clients, I'm going to be honest with you. And sometimes you need to test this out to see if a method really does work and gets results, because sometimes people either are too hard on themselves and it honestly doesn't work, or they're too easy on themselves and they let themselves off the hook, and that doesn't work either. So, I think we need to pay attention to both.

CALL PREP SHEET

I don't make it mandatory for clients to send a call prep sheet to me. Some coaches do. It's kind of like when you have executives who are accustomed to going into meetings and having an agenda that's been sent out prior so that there are talking points and they have a direction that the meeting is going to go. Well, I do the same thing with a call preparation sheet. What this does, basically, is ascertain what they got out of the last session that we had. What has worked for them? What hasn't worked for them? Where have they kind of gotten tripped up? What's come up for them that they really need to focus on? And what would they like this call to be about? So it's not lengthy. It's one page, really simple. But even if they only read the sheet, it has value because it makes them become conscious to what has been going on. It brings them up to speed mentally for the call, or for the session that they're about to be in. Super enlightening, super powerful, very helpful.

RULES OF THE GAME

Next you really want to have a set of "Rules of the Game" you can share. I have seen coaches who have a billion rules, and I have seen those that have three rules. So there's not a rule about how many rules. But here are a few key rules of working together:

1. I want a 24-hour notice of cancellations. I have an electronic scheduler so clients can go in and reschedule or cancel an appointment up to just a minute before the appointment, but I warn them, if I

wasn't given 24 hours of notice I have to charge them for the session, even if simply rescheduling.

2. If a client calls in and I don't answer, they should call right back instead of wasting time leaving a voice message.

These of course are just a few examples, but it's important that you set boundaries for your coaching. Clients respect it, actually. Every executive has boundaries as to how open their door is – whether they are readily available or need appointments to be booked. Coaches are the exactly the same.

SCHEDULING

In terms of scheduling, you want to make sure that you delineate windows of time when you're in business. And not willy-nilly like, "Sunday, Monday, Tuesday, Wednesday," either, as that's too general. I have certain days that I do my coaching. There are many electronic schedulers out there today. I highly recommend that you use one and that you find a system that is beneficial for you, that works according to how you want it to work. It helps keep everybody clear about their time zone, as well (a real factor today in scheduling!).

I do think it's very important that you honor a schedule. I think it's important that when you're on, you're on, and when you're off, you're off. It's important that you have a personal life and prevent disruptions in both your personal and your business affairs. A scheduler, therefore, is one of the premier pieces in your practice. Along with the Target Plan and your emotional state, I would say a schedule is among the top three things that are going to help you be effective and efficient.

Wheels of Life and Business

I send everyone a wheel of life and a wheel of business. Both of these are important because in business they have different categories, or departments, and each of those represents a sliver of pie in the wheel. It's important to look at what's taking their attention. What are the areas of focus in their life? The wheel of life gives them an advance thought about this before I ever meet with them.

Assessments

Then of course, there are assessments. Depending on the clients, I may send assessments before we ever meet or I might send them as we move along. I'm always learning about new assessments and new helpful tools, so as I learn about them I send them out.

CONTACT MANAGEMENT

You might want to have a contact management system to utilize so you can more efficiently and consistently stay in touch and email your clients. There are dozens of them out there. It's a place where you can keep all of your current clients, your past clients, or your employees and past employees. It's your resource center on all the people that you are in touch with and you communicate with on a regular basis. This is a system that can be very important for you.

WEBSITE AND BLOG

As you build your business you will very likely also build a website and a blog. Remember to stay true to your brand in both. If you're blogging, you will want to do that consistently.

RECORDS

It's critical that you've got good records kept for employees or clients, for team members, or whoever you're managing. Electronic records these days are super helpful, but it may be if you've got paper files that you should have a file folder for every client. You should have easy access to that and you should have it systematically set up so that you can access and find their files very easily. You might also want to be sure certain files are kept locked and private. I have seen people need their files because something happened to a client, something went sideways and they needed to get the information from the coach because the coach was the last person somebody talked to, or had the record of what was going on with a person. Generally the files are all confidential, and there are very few extenuating circumstances, but at times the coach can be really helpful because of that file.

FIFTY POWERFUL MARKETING IDEAS

A Neat Ornamented, or Town Coach

THERE ARE UNDOUBTEDLY HUNDREDS of ways to build a coaching business. The primary focus of *The Power of Done* is to give you tools and insights to work with your staff, colleagues, employees, team or clients. But I would be remiss if I didn't also give you some ideas to start, grow, or launch your business. Every coach I know starts coaching because they simply want to help others improve. Very often it begins as helping other colleagues, staff, employees or team members to grow in what they are doing -- or perhaps in my case, to emulate what I had some success in by giving them the tips, secrets and shortcuts to success. Eventually they want to get paid. Coaching is a very lucrative field if you do as I did in my first career and treat it as a business and not a hobby.

PEOPLE YOU KNOW

You will find gold in these next ideas when put into full practice. These are in five simple categories that are intended to jog your thoughts and get you started, and get you into action to make things happen. First there is the entire realm of the people you already know. This is about building one-on-one and using your network:

1. Referrals from family and friends
2. Referrals from past clients
3. Coaching people you know pro bono, making raving fans so they want more, re-enroll, and refer others
4. Marketing to past clients to have them return: make them an offer on another 'level' or other topic

5. Offer a free session to give people a taste of what it is like and what can happen in coaching

6. Contact other experts (respected friends and experts: CPAs, attorneys, therapists) and ask them what would need to happen to be someone they would refer their clients to

7. Contact companies and become the company coach

8. Contact HR departments and ask if you can coach the HR individual personally; ask if you can coach the leaders or a team at the company

9. Call local business owners and offer to help them take their business to the next level

10. Play the "Card Game": put 20 business cards in your pocket and hand them out with your "elevator pitch," giving people an opportunity to have you help them grow, expand, shift, or change their life and business

EXISTING RELATIONSHIPS

Second is tapping into all the relationships you already have:

11. Be conscious with every acquaintance you make. Our world is no longer six degrees separated. Your relationships are filled with possible clients.

12. Take coaching continuing education courses. Learning new skills and tools sets you apart and gives you a reason for people to hire you instead of someone else. In meeting people at the classes, often you have a skill they need and you will find clients in the class. I've coached the *teachers* in some of the courses, as well.

13. Join professional organizations, like the International Coach Federation. Become active in the local chapters. Coaches believe in coaching and will hire you to coach them.

14. Join the National Speakers Association or Toastmasters International. Speakers need a coach and coaches raise their game when they are effective speakers.

15. Become a member of networking groups. This is a great place to be a referral source and receive referrals and meet engaging professionals.

16. Be active in your local chamber of commerce as well as visiting others when you travel. You will make new friends who might need your service,

so spare one more lonely night in a strange city in a hotel room.

17. Join organizations such as women's' or men's' groups or service organizations. For example, the Lions, Rotary, Kiwanis clubs.

18. Offer your services to career counseling companies and services. Offer to coach the staff and their recruits. It makes them more hirable.

19. Participate in seminars of all kinds, particularly personal development seminars. Your next clients are sitting right next to you!

20. Join and be active in clubs that are involved in something you enjoy. There are organizations for everything—knitting, biking, hiking, bible study, triathlons, yoga, you name it. You will find clients and wonderful referrals from people that you share an interest with.

TRADITIONAL MEDIA

Third is to use traditional media. Often what was old is now new again!

21. Write a book and eBook! Be a published author.

22. Use a publicist. They will get your name in the news and print in interviews in traditional media.

23. Create and post press releases about every little thing that could possibly be new.

24. Become the "expert" on your local radio.

25. Become the "expert" on your specialty (create one) on television.

26. Write articles and expose them to every type of print. For example, in-flight magazines are looking for articles all the time.

27. Send your entire address book an invitation to something you are offering, be it an article, CD, DVD, or download. Ask them for a referral and (via email) keep asking!

28. Advertise in your local newspapers.

29. Advertise where you do business, your health clubs, country club, and community notice boards.

30. Send out postcards or emails with a brief, uplifting message and invitation to have a sample session.

TECHNOLOGY

Fourth is the area that everyone seems to be in and is critical to use—technology:

31. Have a website that reflects who you are as a coach and what you offer to clients. Keep it up-to-date and relevant. Be sure you have a way for clients to reach you through your site.

32. Link to related or educational sites.

33. Collect names and emails and develop your *tribe*. Interact with them often. Everyone you know and meet should be on your list!

34. Send free links, downloads, and articles to your tribe regularly.

35. Give an eBook or chapters of your book to people who are showing up at your site.

36. Actively blog on your website. Engaging and useful writings and video will create a tribe that wants to interact and will want more of you.

37. Email a newsletter to your list. Have your current newsletter on your website available for download.

38. Build a list *purposely*. Ask everyone you meet at organizations, seminars, network meetings for

their email information and tell them you have some great things you would love to send them free.

39. Podcast! Create your own radio show and share your coaching tips. People having an experience of you will want you one-on-one.

40. Tele-summit! Create an interview version of your podcast or webinar. You would be surprised who will say yes to an interview. To be honest, I have never been told no!

SOCIAL MEDIA

Fifth is today's favorite, social media:

41. Facebook

42. Twitter

43. Tumblr

44. Instagram

45. YouTube

46. Blog (video or written)

47. Guest posts on others' Facebook, blogs, websites, as long as you share an audience/demographic/avatar.

48. Podcast

49. Share others' content on your blog, Facebook, and other social media.

50. "OPM," or "Other People's Media" links to your audience.

BONUS IDEA!

The last idea I like to call the BONUS IDEA! It's actually the *number one* thing to do, the number one idea of all, and that's to FOLLOW UP! Every person you meet could be a potential client or they will know someone that could really use your assistance. You must follow up with them and remind them that when you spoke you really were serious and you really do want to help. You *do* have strategies and ideas and probing questions to get to the bottom of what is happening with them and to help them come to solutions and resolutions to whatever it is they need answers for.

Along with that I would say—or if you ask or say nothing else be ready to ask, "Who do you know that could use some assistance in growing, expanding, changing, shifting, or eliminating something in their life?" That alone can be the opening of a long relationship in coaching with an individual, a team, or a company.

Prior to launching all your brilliant marketing and clever ideas you will want to be clear of who you are as a coach. You will want to have done the exercises and created a powerful identity with clear beliefs and values that substantiate all your promises and platform you stand on. Individuals, teams and companies will place their futures in your hands and you will want to have all the certainty there is that you are the one that is the right to do it with them, that you are the one to change their lives and businesses by sharing the *Power of Done*!

Now go succeed, make others succeed, and tell me about it!

GET YOUR FREE BONUS!

In appreciation of your buying and reading this book, and as an encouragement of your success as a coach and in your life, please accept these free bonuses I have arranged for you.

Visit this page today!

http://www.cynthiafreeman.com/get-your-free-bonus/

PART 5: RESOURCES

FIVE STAR FORMULA

PHYSIOLOGY
- WALK
- TALK
- STANCE
- BREATH
- FACE EXPRESSION

SELF-TALK
- WHAT ARE YOU SAYING TO YOURSELF?

BELIEFS
- WHAT DO YOU BELIEVE ABOUT THAT?

FOCUS
- WHAT ARE YOU THINKING ABOUT?
- WHAT ARE YOU FOCUSED ON?

MEANINGS YOU MAKE UP
- WHAT ARE YOU MAKING THINGS MEAN?
- "SO WHAT"

For more useful coaching resources please visit
www.CynthiaFreeman.com

7-Step Powerful Coaching Sessions

1) CONNECT
   - Get into rapport
   - Relate to who they are what they might have been doing
   - "Take the temperature"
   - Where are they 1-10
2) CHECK-IN
   - What did they apply since the last call?
   - What worked?
   - What progress did they make?
   - What didn't work? (make a note…discussing why or what was in the way use in step 4/5)
3) CELEBRATE WINS
   - Any progress, any application is a win
   - Notice any tiny movement forward
   - Celebrate this progress as a new piece of their identity
   - Cheer, pat on the back clapping
4) CLARIFY OUTCOME
   - Based on progress what is their next step
   - If they didn't make progress set as a part of the outcome what obstacles are in the way?
   - Set as outcome of the call next forward motion
   - If they have made progress this is a good time to add another area of focus as a n outcome
5) COACH USING ULTIMATE COACH STRATEGIES

- What strategies does this client need to move them in a forward direction?
- Five Star Formula
- Active listening/6HN/Love languages/meta-programs
- Life/Business Wheel/Ultimate Game/Sales Game/Inner Team
- Assessments

6) CREATE PLAN OF ACTION
   - Set target
   - Get leverage and clear motives for why the client will achieve it
   - What are the actions they COULD take to achieve it?
   - What is the 20 percent to hit the target most effectively and efficiently?
   - Schedule the key actions

7) CONDTION AND COMMIT
   - Anchor/Incantation/Repetition

For more useful coaching resources please visit
www.CynthiaFreeman.com

RULES OF THE GAME

1. The relationship you have with your coach is a partnership. Your coach is an outstanding professional, whose sole focus is to empower you to attain the results you desire. In order to achieve the results you deserve, you must do your part by following through on the commitments you make. These commitments include showing up for every scheduled coaching session and completing any action items that you have committed to between sessions.

2. Your coach has a 24 hour cancellation policy. Much like a doctor's or dentist's office, if you reschedule more than 24 hours in advance, everything proceeds as normal. If you need to reschedule less than 24 hours in advance, or worse case, you completely forget a coaching call, the call will be considered a completed session and will be counted towards your coaching plan.

3. Per your agreement, your coaching sessions are up to 30 minutes in length. To utilize your coaching to the fullest extent make sure to call your coach promptly

at the designated session time. If you call in late for your appointment, your session will still conclude at the original session completion time and will count as a completed session.

4. Call your coach at the telephone number listed above. If the coach is not available when you call please leave a confidential message for them. If it is your designated call time please call again in one minute. Your coach is expecting you and expecting you to call.

5. When conducting a coaching call, ensure you are doing it from an environment in which you will be able to totally concentrate and focus (free from interruptions). It is also important that you have privacy so that you are able to say whatever you need to say (i.e. speak your truth).

6. Coaching is not *therapy* and you will not be doing any therapy as part of the coaching program. We define therapy as working on the past. Our focus in your coaching is getting results in both the present and the future.

PREPARING FOR YOUR FIRST CALL

Complete your questionnaire and information fact sheet and return them via email (preferred) or fax prior to your call allowing time for your coach to read and prepare for your call.

Have a copy of your questions with you for your call. It is an excellent idea to have a blank book, journal, or spiral notebook for your coaching calls. This allows you to capture notes, thoughts and assignments and keep it all in one place.

For more useful coaching resources please visit
www.CynthiaFreeman.com

PLANNING COACHING CALLS

Coach: _____

Client: _____

Call Date & Time: _____

Specific, measurable actions I committed to on my last call:

- _____
- _____
- _____

Actions I have taken since my last call (Be sure you address each commitment made whether taken or not and to what degree.):

- _____
- _____
- _____

New opportunities and positive result(s) of actions taken (What benefits did I gain from my action?):

- _____
- _____
- _____

Challenges experienced and/or lessons learned since last call:

- _____

- _____

- _____

- _____

Outcomes for next call (What do you need from this call to move you forward on your goals?):

- _____

- _____

- _____

For more useful coaching resources please visit
www.CynthiaFreeman.com

7 KEYS OF COACHING, "CREATE IT"

Step 1. Create RELATIONSHIP.

- Build rapport
- Active listening
- Mirror/match
- Compassion/authenticity

Step 2. Explore WHO they are.

- Discover their background, culture, education
- Needs, values, beliefs
- Significant emotional event
- What are they looking for?

Step 3. Assess WHY they make the choices they do.

- Wheel of Life/Business
- Stress Scale/Love Languages/Personalities/Strengths and Limitations
- What's Important? What do they think about? What do they focus on?
- How do they meet their needs?
- Who do they say they are?

Step 4. Transform VALUES/BELIEFS/IDENTITY RECONSTRUCTION

- Five Star Formula:
    1. Physiology,
    2. Self Talk,
    3. Beliefs,
    4. Focus,
    5. Meaning
- Quality questions
- Build strengths
- Create new values, beliefs, identity

Step 5. EXECUTION and IMPLEMENTATION: Design a Plan and take Right Action

- RRR (Results, Reasons, Roadmap)
- Clear result
- Dozens of reasons for leverage and motives
- Actions to get to the result, 20%/80%, Schedule

Step 6. INTEGRATE and CELEBRATE!

- Rehearse, condition to Integrate the new ways of being

- Incantations/Anchoring
- Commit to when and how often to create new habit
- Celebrate the commitment and future success

Step 7 Take the NEXT STEP and build MOMENTUM

- Define the NEXT LEVEL
- Build on momentum
- Make it sustainable

Your clients want a result; your invitation as their coach is to partner with them to CREATE IT!

~

For more useful coaching resources please visit
www.CynthiaFreeman.com

QUESTIONNAIRE & AGREEMENT

**COACHING COMPANY
COACH NAME
COACH'S ADDRESS
COACH PHONE NUMBER**

Date: _____

Dear <<Client>>,

Congratulations on your commitment to design your life exactly the way you want it! I am really looking forward to working with you. I feel confident that some exciting outcomes will be created through our designed alliance and our coaching relationship.

Attached is a questionnaire for you to **review and complete as best you can prior to our initial session (completion is NOT a requirement for beginning coaching sessions).** Please fax or email the enclosed questionnaire back to me as soon as you complete it. (Please forward the information sheet and agreement ***PRIOR*** to your initial coaching session.)

Feel free to call if you have any questions. It will be an honor and a privilege to partner with you as you choose to live your life using your unique talents, being deliberate about designing your future—you truly are a leader!

Warmest regards and to your greatest success,

<<Coach Name>>

P.S.: I've attached a special "Rules of the Game" that you will find helpful to maximize your coaching experience. Please read this prior to your first coaching session.

PERSONAL INFORMATION FACT SHEET

All information is treated confidential

Full Name:

Mailing Address:

Home Phone #:

Work Phone #:

Fax #:

Cell Phone #:

E-Mail Address:

Occupation—What you're doing now for a living:

Employer Name:

Employer Address:

Date of Birth:

Marital Status:

Significant Others' Name:

SO's date of birth:

Wedding or Special Anniversary:

Children's Names and Ages:

CLIENT QUESTIONNAIRE

PLEASE TAKE TIME TO THINK ABOUT THE FOLLOWING QUESTIONS AND YOUR RESPONSES. THE MORE CLEARLY AND THOUGHTFULLY YOU ANSWER THESE QUESTIONS, THE MORE PRODUCTIVE OUR WORK WILL BE TOGETHER.

1.   What events or accomplishments must occur in your lifetime for you to feel satisfied and have few, if any, regrets?

2.   What are you passionate about? What gets your blood pumping? This can be actual or still in the "dream" stage.

3.   Do you have a secret passion? It can be some action or idea that is too exciting to act on or grow further. Tell me about it.

4.   What kinds of roles do you see yourself having in the following areas: Your local community, your Country, the world?

5.   Assuming your lifestyle and money were constant, what would you devote your life/time to? Describe the circumstances you would operate under.

6.   For you to be coached most effectively, what do I need to know about you?

7.   If you had a five-year goal and the continuing services of a coach to help you achieve it, what goal would that be?

8.   What is missing from your life that would make it more fulfilling?

9.   Do you believe in God or a High Power/Great Spirit, etc. Please describe the points of your beliefs/relationship that are the most helpful for strengthening you?

10.   What is your life purpose? How do you use this vision in your daily living? How do you know it is right for you?

11.   Are there any other areas you would like me to know about you?

CATEGORIES OF LIFE

Please list, prioritize, and rate from 0-10 each of the categories of focus or interest in your life (10 being that there is NO room for improvement in that category and 0 meaning it needs help desperately) Examples of categories: career, intimate relationship, finances, health, spiritual, family & friends, travel and leisure, lifestyle, other.

1.

2.

3.

4.

5.

7.

8.

OTHER AREAS OF INTEREST

What are the three most important things in your life?

What behaviors or habits are still showing up in your life in a way that doesn't serve you well?

What are your blind spots or hot buttons that keep you from success?

What patterns of sabotage keep repeating?

What challenges/lessons do you continually find yourself confronted with?

Can you think of anything else that stands in your way of success?

PRIMARY FOCUS

Please list 3–5 areas that you would like to be our PRIMARY area of focus in our work together!

1.

2.

3.

4.

5.

How would you know that you had had success in these areas?

1.

2.

3.

4.

5.

COACHING AGREEMENT

This agreement, between COACH'S NAME AND/OR COMPANY and Client will begin on Date and will continue for a minimum of three months. The monthly coaching rate will be billed at $000 per month for the first 3 months for 2 one full hour sessions payable in advance each month and 2 touch base phone calls as needed and a HOTSHEET for target tracking . We will have the option to renew the agreement at that time. You may place a credit card on file and have the amount be automatically billed on the first of each month. Please fill out the information on the bottom of this agreement and email or fax it to COACH'S NAME AND /OR COMPANY.

The services to be provided by COACH'S NAME AND/OR COMPANY to the client are coaching or tele-coaching, as designed jointly with the client. Coaching, which is not advice, therapy or counseling, may address specific personal projects, business successes or general conditions in the client's life or profession. Other coaching services include values clarification, brainstorming, identifying plans (including appropriate action steps to support their fulfillment), examining modes of operating in life, asking clarifying questions and making empowering requests, as well as tools to assist in creating change.

Upon completion of the three months, COACH'S NAME AND/OR COMPANY coaching may convert to a month-to-month basis. The client and COACH'S NAME coach agree to provide one another with a 30-Day Notice to cancel further services. The client will call COACH at the weekly scheduled time. Twenty-four (24) hour notice is required to cancel or reschedule an appointment.

COACH'S NAME AND/ OR COMPANY promises the above named client that all information provided to COACH'S NAME AND/OR COMPANY will be kept strictly confidential. We know that we will be asking for explicit and specific personal information; we respect your willingness to be truthful, and we will treat this information as a special confidence.

Throughout our working relationship we will continue to engage in very direct and personal conversations. You can count on us to be honest and straight forward, asking questions and making requests. The purpose of our interaction is to remind the client of the initial intention and to coach the client to realize those intentions. The client firmly understands that in order for this coaching relationship be powerful, they must take full responsibility for granting it power and do just that --- have the coaching relationship be powerful. When the client sees coaching not working as desired, the client will communicate and take actions to once again return the power to the coaching relationship.

Your return of this contract via email will constitute acceptance in lieu of a signature.

CREDIT CARD #: _____

EXP DATE: _____/_____

Name as it appears on card: _____

Billing address: _____

_____

_____

For more useful coaching resources please visit
www.CynthiaFreeman.com

WHEEL OF LIFE

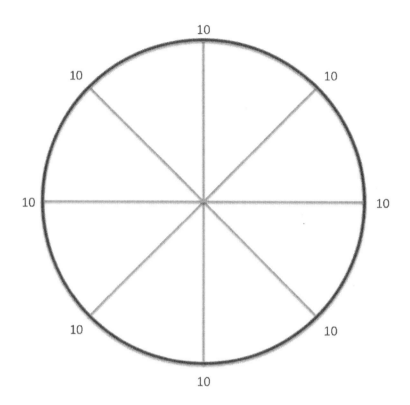

TARGET PLAN

Dynamic Life Target Planning

Target/Objective:_____ Date when:_____

Menu of Options	Motive, Leverage & Reasons Why

Menu of Options

1. How can I make this target happen?

   What are **ALL** the things I **COULD** do to achieve this target?

   (Answer this until there are no additional answers.)

	By when?

2. Asterisk (·) the 20% that will most likely achieve 80% of the result.
3. Schedule the 20% items.
4. Review weekly and update.

Motive, Leverage & Reasons Why
Categories of Questions

1. Why is this Target a must? Why is it important?

2. What will...this target give me?
   ...it allow me to do?
   ...I gain if I achieve this?

3. What will...it cost if I do not achieve this?
   ...I lose?
   ...I not be able to do?

4. How will I feel when I have hit the target? What will it mean to me?

Dynamic Life – Cynthia Freeman – PO Box 1001 – Newport Beach, CA 92659 – (949) 642-7200

HOT SHEET / ACTION TRACKER

Week Of: _____

Hot Sheet Action Tracker For: _____

Category	1 Year Outcome	#1 Leverage	20% >>>> 80%	Week Outcome

PERSONALITY PROFILE

WHO ARE YOU?

Here are some suggestions that will assist you in completing the profile:

1. Unless otherwise directed, answer every question from your earliest recollections of how you were as a child. Since your personality is innate and comes with your soul, this will provide a more accurate perspective on who you innately are as opposed to who you have become.

2. At first, mark the choices that come to you most readily. Skip the more difficult questions, but return to them later.

3. Do not hesitate to ask others for feedback—especially people who may not agree with you. Their opinions can help you balance your self-assessment.

4. Strive to choose answers that are most often typical of your thoughts and/or actions. Subconsciously, you may want to avoid identifying—or facing—the real you, but think

it out. Don't cheat yourself by prettying things up. The potential rewards for honesty are too great.

5. Some of you may consciously seek ways to "beat" the profile and actually look for patterns in order to skew the profile results. Others may perceive the profile design to be oversimplified. I caution you not to be fooled. The profile has been successfully used by hundreds of thousands of readers for over ten years in producing reliable insights. The results have reinforced my confidence that your honesty and the profile's simplicity are a tough team to beat.

Directions: Mark an "X" by the one word or phrase that best describes what you are like most of the time. Choose only one response from each group.

	CEO **CHOLERIC** **POWERFUL** **YELLOW**	**ENGINEER** **MELANCHOLY** **PERFECT** **BLUE**	**AMBASSADOR** **PHLEGMATIC** **PEACEFUL** **WHITE**	**ACTOR** **SANGUINE** **POPULAR** **RED**
1	__ Conceited	__ Supportive	__ Dry wit	__ Outgoing
2	__ Authoritative	__ Perfectionist	__ Vacillates	__ Self-centered
3	__ Dominant	__ Sympathetic	__ Lenient	__ Enthusiastic
4	__ Self-serving	__ Suspicious	__ Unsure	__ Naïve
5	__ Decisive	__ Loyal	__ Contented	__ Playful
6	__ Arrogant	__ Worry prone	__ Will of iron	__ Flighty
7	__ Assertive	__ Reliable	__ Kind	__ Spontaneous
8	__ Brash	__ Self-judging	__ Reluctant	__ Teaches
9	__ Action-oriented	__ Analytical	__ Easygoing	__ Indiscreet
10	__ Critical of others	__ Overly sensitive	__ Shy	__ Obnoxious
11	__ Undeterred	__ Detailed	__ A good listener	__ Hospitable
12	__ Demanding	__ Unforgiving	__ Unmotivated	__ Vain
13	__ Duty-driven	__ Idealistic	__ Considerate	__ Happy
14	__ Impatient	__ Gloomy	__ Bystander	__ Impatient
15	__ Strong-willed	__ Respectful	__ Patient	__ Fun-loving
16	__ Argumentative	__ Unreachable	__ Directionless	__ Interrupts
17	__ Independent	__ Dependable	__ Conciliatory	__ Trusting
18	__ Bullish	__ Sad	__ Uncertain	__ Forgetful
19	__ Powerful	__ Deliberate	__ Bland	__ Optimistic
20	__ Insensitive	__ Judgmental	__ Boring	__ Undisciplined
21	__ Logical	__ Anxious	__ Agreeable	__ Popular
22	__ Right	__ Self-accusing	__ Unenthusiastic	__ Uncommitted
23	__ Dogmatic	__ Mannered	__ Accepting	__ Passionate
24	__ Merciless	__ Sensible	__ Detached	__ Prankster
25	__ Task-oriented	__ Conscientious	__ Diplomatic	__ Fiery
26	__ Tactless	__ Critical	__ Lazy	__ Loud
27	__ Blunt	__ Creative	__ Adaptable	__ Performer
28	__ Calculating	__ Self-righteous	__ Self-deprecating	__ Disorganized
29	__ Confident	__ Disciplined	__ Pleasant	__ Charismatic
30	__ Bulldozer	__ Calculated	__ Unproductive	__ Truth-denier
31	__ Adventurous	__ Analytical	__ Adaptable	__ Animated
32	__ Persuasive	__ Persistent	__ Peaceful	__ Flirt
33	__ Headstrong	__ Martyr	__ Obedient	__ Gregarious
34	__ Competitive	__ Considerate	__ Controlled	__ Convincing
35	__ Resourceful	__ Respectful	__ Removed	__ Refreshing

CEO CHOLERIC POWERFUL YELLOW	ENGINEER MELANCHOLY PERFECT BLUE	AMBASSADOR PHLEGMATIC PEACEFUL WHITE	ACTOR SANGUINE POPULAR RED

	CEO	ENGINEER	AMBASSADOR	ACTOR
36	__ Self-reliant	__ Sensitive	__ Satisfied	__ Spirited
37	__ Positive	__ Planner	__ Patient	__ Encourager
38	__ Infallible	__ Scheduled	__ Shy	__ Spontaneous
39	__ Outspoken	__ Orderly	__ Polite	__ Optimistic
40	__ Forceful	__ Legalistic	__ Friendly	__ Jolly
41	__ Daring	__ Detailed	__ Diplomatic	__ Delightful
42	__ Strong	__ Cultured	__ Consistent	__ Friendly
43	__ Independent	__ Idealistic	__ Inoffensive	__ Inspiring
44	__ Decisive	__ Deep	__ Calm	__ Effervescent
45	__ Right	__ Musical	__ Mediator	__ Mixes easily
46	__ Tenacious	__ Thoughtful	__ Tolerant	__ Chatty
47	__ Leader	__ Loyal	__ Listener	__ Light-hearted
48	__ Captain	__ Chart maker	__ Contented	__ Cute
49	__ Productive	__ Mathematical	__ Pleasant	__ Popular
50	__ Bold	__ Rules follower	__ Harmonious	__ Spirited
51	__ Bossy	__ Bashful	__ Vacant	__ Brazen
52	__ Intolerant	__ Holds grudges	__ Unenthusiastic	__ Undisciplined
53	__ Resistant	__ Bitter	__ Un-wordy	__ Repetitious
54	__ Direct	__ Finicky	__ Fearful	__ Forgetful
55	__ Impatient	__ Insecure	__ Indecisive	__ Interrupts
56	__ Unaffectionate	__ Unpopular	__ Uninvolved	__ Unscheduled
57	__ Directive	__ Rigid	__ Hesitant	__ Careless
58	__ Proud	__ Pessimistic	__ Plain	__ Permissive
59	__ Argumentative	__ Disconnected	__ Aimless	__ Angered easily
60	__ Bully	__ Naysayer	__ Noncommittal	__ Naïve
61	__ Workaholic	__ Withdrawn	__ Anxious	__ Desires credit
62	__ Tactless	__ Temperamental	__ Timid	__ Talkative
63	__ Tyrannical	__ Depressed	__ Doubtful	__ Disorganized
64	__ Intolerant	__ Introvert	__ Indifferent	__ Inconsistent
65	__ Manipulative	__ Moody	__ Speechless	__ Messy
66	__ Stubborn	__ Skeptical	__ Slow	__ Flamboyant
67	__ Talks-over-others	__ Loner	__ Lazy	__ Loud
68	__ Short tempered	__ Incriminating	__ Listless	__ Giddy
69	__ Audacious	__ Revengeful	__ Passive	__ Restless
70	__ Crafty	__ Particular	__ Compromising	__ Compulsive

PERSONALITY IN PERSPECTIVE

Enter your totals in the proper spaces. Now let's see if you respond the same way to the following situations as you did to groups of descriptive words. Again, pick only one answer, and record your totals for each letter at the end of the section.

SITUATIONS

1. If I applied for a job, a prospective employer would most likely hire me because I am:
    a. Driven, direct, and delegating.
    b. Deliberate, accurate and reliable.
    c. Patient, adaptable, and tactful.
    d. Fun-loving, spirited and casual.

2. When involved in an intimate relationship, if I feel threatened by my partner, I:
    a. Fight back with facts and anger.
    b. Cry, feel hurt, and plan revenge.
    c. Become quiet, withdrawn, and often hold anger until I blow up over some minor issue later.
    d. Distance myself and avoid further conflict.

3. For me, life is most meaningful when it:
    a. Is task-oriented and productive.
    b. Is filled with people and purpose.
    c. Is free of pressure and stress.

    d. Allows me to be playful, lighthearted, and optimistic.

4. As a child, I was:
    a. Stubborn, bright and/or aggressive.
    b. Well-behaved, caring, and/or depressed.
    c. Quiet, easygoing, and/or shy.
    d. Too talkative, happy, and/or playful.

5. As an adult, I am:
    a. Opinionated, determined, and/or bossy.
    b. Responsible, honest, and/or unforgiving.
    c. Accepting, contented, and/or unmotivated.
    d. Charismatic, positive, and/or obnoxious.

6. As a parent, I am:
    a. Demanding, quick-tempered, and/or uncompromising.
    b. Concerned, sensitive, and/or critical.
    c. Permissive, easily persuaded, and/or often overwhelmed.
    d. Playful, casual, and/or irresponsible.

7. In an argument with a friend, I am most likely to be:
    a. Verbally stubborn about facts.
    b. Concerned about others feelings and principles.
    c. Silently stubborn, uncomfortable, and/or confused.
    d. Loud, uncomfortable, and/or compromising.

8. If my friend was in trouble, I would be:
   a. Protective, resourceful, and recommend solutions.
   b. Concerned, empathetic, and loyal—regardless of the problem.
   c. Supportive, patient, and a good listener.
   d. Nonjudgmental, optimistic, and downplaying the seriousness of the situation.

9. When making decisions, I am:
   a. Assertive, articulate, and logical.
   b. Deliberate, precise, and cautious.
   c. Indecisive, timid, and reluctant.
   d. Impulsive, uncommitted, and inconsistent.

10. When I fail, I feel:
    a. Silently self-critical, yet verbally stubborn and defensive.
    b. Guilty, self-critical, and vulnerable to depression—I dwell on it.
    c. Unsettled and fearful, but I keep it to myself.
    d. Embarrassed and nervous—seeking to escape the situation.

11. If someone crosses me:
    a. I am angered, and cunningly plan ways to get even quickly.
    b. I feel deeply hurt and find it almost impossible to forgive completely. Generally, getting even is not enough.

   c. I am silently hurt and plan to get even and/or completely avoid the other person.

   d. I want to avoid confrontation, consider the situation not important.

12. Work is:

   a. A most productive way to spend one's time.

   b. A healthy activity, which should be done right if it's to be done as all. Work should be done before one plays.

   c. A positive activity as long as it is something I enjoy and don't feel pressured to accomplish.

   d. A necessary evil, much less inviting than play.

13. In social situations, I am most often:

   a. Feared by others.

   b. Admired by others.

   c. Protected by others.

   d. Envied by others.

14. In a relationship, I am most concerned with being:

   a. Approved of and right.

   b. Understood, appreciated, and intimate.

   c. Respected, tolerant, and peaceful

   d. Praised, having fun, and feeling free.

15. To feel alive and positive, I seek:

   a. Adventure, leadership, and lots of action.

   b. Security, creativity, and purpose.

   c. Acceptance and safety.

d. Excitement, playful productivity, and the company of others.

For more useful coaching resources please visit www.CynthiaFreeman.com

Acknowledgements

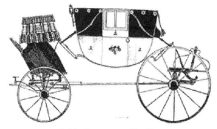

Through the many years of my pursuit of personal development, dozens of teachers and trainers have coached, mentored, influenced and shaped me into who I have become, as have 24 years of clients who listened and grew, and were a part of the processional effect of growth and change—always willing to try new tools and experiment along with me. I thank them all.

In specific, thanks to:

Rick Warren

Tony Robbins

Joseph McClendon III

Roger Love

Tom McCarthy

Ed Rush

Florence Littauer

Emily Barnes

Pam Hendrickson

Mike Koenigs

All of you have had such a profound influence on me both personally and professionally—these few words are inadequate.

Thanks also to Rodney Miles, my other brain, who spent so much time and *patience* getting this book out of me and into your hands, and our esteemed editor, Dana Nichols, insuring the book could be easily read and understood.

For Scott Harris, gratitude for causing me to put 24 years of my experience into some sort of order—semblance of order, anyway! Sincere gratitude. You were the cause, and this book is the effect.

Thanks to Brittany and David, my beloved children, who were my first "clients." They are supreme examples of making amazing things happen as they both have climbed poles, broken boards, walked on fire, and created their lives the way they designed them to be.

Thanks to my Mastermind Retreat Group (you know who you are!). They have been my cheerleaders, advisors and compatriots throughout this process.

And to the many who have and will be influenced by the coaches and clients I have and will coach, I wish them empowerment along with rich, fulfilled lives.

ABOUT CYNTHIA FREEMAN

CYNTHIA FREEMAN is a coaching pioneer. A master certified coach and veteran of over 22 years of coaching experience, she has worked with over 2,400 clients including AT&T, MTV, Cisco, House of Blues, Dutch Bro's Coffee,  Disney, and thousands of small business owners and entrepreneurs.

A sought after seminar speaker, she has presented in front of audiences as large as 17,000 and shared the stage with such speakers as Larry King, Tony Robbins, Tom Hopkins, Og Mandino, Florence Littauer, and Emily Barnes.

Cynthia has accomplished all of this while maintaining a family-friendly lifestyle. Even when closing over 200 real estate deals a year with six full-time assistants, she never worked weekends, she took 10 weeks off per year, and fully participated in the lives and educations of her two children. People started asking Cynthia to coach them to grow their income while not sacrificing their lives or families.

She is one of the few who can say that they have exceeded the half of 1 percent in *two* careers, and more than 2,400 clients later, she still has a passion for helping business owners and entrepreneurs to make more money while taking more time off to live more vibrant lives.

GET YOUR FREE BONUS!

In appreciation of your buying and reading this book, and as an encouragement of your success as a coach and in your life, please accept these free bonuses I have arranged for you. Visit this page today!

http://www.cynthiafreeman.com/get-your-free-bonus/